Praise for
I Can't Rest Now, Lord! I'm Responsible...
by Gena Bradford

"To all of you who feel the weight of the world bearing down on your shoulders… STOP right now and READ this book! You are not responsible for everything and everyone. Jesus is! Gena Bradford reminds us in this delightful (and helpful) book that Jesus is responsible, and we only need to be responsive to Him. Through Gena's honest reflections on her own journey, you'll learn to let go, trust more, and open up to God's best for you!"

—*Joe Wittwer:* Lead Pastor of Life Center Church in Spokane, WA

"I was blessed by the richness in truth of Gena's personal experience stories and how they paralleled God's Word so clearly. Through this devotional study, *I Can't Rest Now, Lord! I'm Responsible...,* I felt completely loved by the Father and His care for me. The principles and teachings resonated deep within my heart, and will help me in years to come. This book is timely, inspiring, and a cool drink in the busyness of daily life and ministry."

—*Faith Orr:* wife, mother, and school principal

"I am the sole provider for my family, and my job can be emotionally stressful. Before starting this book study, *I Can't Rest Now, Lord! I'm Responsible...,* I could feel the heaviness of burnout starting to take its toll on my body and mind. Now, I am learning to take on only what I see Christ showing me. I have started making time for creativity through painting, and God gave me the idea to do one fun adventure each month and to invite others to join me. Now, I don't have to feel guilty about doing something new, fun, or relaxing. On Day 14 of the book I embraced the truth of God's love: 'The only way I can fail God is to not let Him love me.' This book is a treasure chest of the rest and delight God wants to share with every believer!"

—*Sharon Hengy:* Residential Services Director of Life Services of Spokane, mother, grandmother, wife and caregiver for disabled husband.

"I have had the wonderful privilege of reading Gena Bradford's book of devotions two times now, and it only gets richer and more impactful. Serving as a pastor's wife, I was grateful to be with 26 women who read and participated in this six-week study. Even those who have not been to the point of true burnout, can greatly benefit from the Biblical principles and revelatory insight Gena has shared with both transparency and poignancy. I believe this study will bless, delight and bring transformation in the hearts of those who read and receive from its timeless truth."
—*Patricia Malott:* women's pastor, wife, mother, and grandmother

"As a retired pastor, I am aware of the common struggle we all have with trying to earn our 'right standing' with God, rather than just receiving His salvation, grace, and love: all because of who He is. Gena, in her book, *I Can't Rest Now, Lord! I'm Responsible...*, does a good job of combining her own personal experiences with the overcoming power of Biblical truths. She provides good practical lessons that help the reader apply the truth of scripture with a daily 'restercise' application, along with prayer, and relative questions."
—*Pastor Denny Klaja*

"Gena's book study was amazingly timed as my husband, Denny, and I were going on be on a month-long trip. It was a blessing to do one lesson almost every day of our trip. I appreciated her candor, vulnerability, and transparency coupled with hope and promise from God's Word! Her study brought me to the forefront of the importance of looking at my motives for why I do things, making sure guilt and obligation are not what's directing my steps. I also appreciated her insight on freedom from regret. My new slogan is: "If it's not light, it's not right!" from Day 9 of her book."
—*Linda Klaja:* pastor's wife and retired school secretary

"This book is not just about resting from activities, but about finding true rest from God, recognizing the true source of unrest, and letting God heal it. This book made me realize it's okay to take care of myself, to please God alone, and to have permission to find ways to be happy and joyful! I am important and so are my dreams."
—*Jeanie Padula:* ultrasound technician, wife, and mother of two

"This devotional book has been a true blessing to me. It's a 'must-read' for every woman suffering from burnout. I highly recommend it! There are many key lessons I'll remember. My hope is that this book makes it into the hands of everyone who is dealing with burnout, and that it becomes a resource to be read and reread every six months."
—*Karen Malone:* wife, mother, a grandmother, and a full-time caregiver for her mother

"Not only would I recommend Gena's book to others, I've already thought of several friends to whom I'd give a copy. This book goes straight to the heart of an epidemic issue that plagues women in our fast-paced, performance-based society. With heartfelt candor, she shares her gut-wrenching experience with burnout, depression, and subsequent health collapse that led her to resign from her job at the zenith of her career. *I Can't Rest Now, Lord! I'm Responsible...*, takes a hard look at the fear-based decisions women make, and offers them both hope and practical help to break out of that cycle, to live the life God intends for them."
—*Evelyn Ainley:* company account manager, wife, mother, and grandmother

"Gena's book, *I Can't Rest Now, Lord! I'm Responsible...*, reveals the reality of the destructive things men and women commonly do to themselves. Not enough is taught on rest. This book is packed full of ideas on how to make significant changes in our lives that bring health, well-being, and joy. By applying the key truths and insights revealed in each of Gena's life lessons, God reminded me, grounded me, and convicted me to stop my fast-paced busy life to enjoy Him and His beauty—He is life abundant. I hope this book reaches many people."
—*Malynda Turner:* business school teacher, wife, mother, and grandmother

"Gena's stories, interwoven with insight, scripture, prayer, and restercise activities, have the power to transform individuals and communities. My hope for this book is that her stories will help others as they did me both personally and professionally. I highly recommend this book to anyone."
—*Rebecca Buchanan:* Doctorate in Spiritual/Human Development, artist, mother, and grandmother

WOMEN'S AND MEN'S DEVOTIONAL
For Individuals (30 Day Format) or Groups (Six to Eight Weeks)

I Can't Rest Now, Lord! I'm Responsible...

30 Days from Burnout to the Heart of God

Gena Bradford

I Can't Rest Now, Lord! I'm Responsible…
©2019 by Gena Bradford

All Rights Reserved.
This book or any portion thereof may not be reproduced or used in any manner whatsoever without the express written permission of the publisher except for the use of brief quotations in a book review.

ISBN: 9781072677062

Scriptures marked AMP are taken from the AMPLIFIED BIBLE (AMP): Scripture taken from the AMPLIFIED® BIBLE, Copyright © 1954, 1958, 1962, 1964, 1965, 1987 by the Lockman Foundation Used by Permission. (www.Lockman.org)

Scriptures marked KJV are taken from the KING JAMES VERSION (KJV): KING JAMES VERSION, public domain.

Scriptures marked TM are taken from the THE MESSAGE: THE BIBLE IN CONTEMPORARY ENGLISH (TM): Scripture taken from THE MESSAGE: THE BIBLE IN CONTEMPORARY ENGLISH, copyright©1993, 1994, 1995, 1996, 2000, 2001, 2002. Used by permission of NavPress Publishing Group.

Scriptures marked TMNIV are taken from the Holy Bible, NEW INTERNATIONAL VERSION®, NIV® Copyright © 1973, 1978, 1984, 2011 by Biblica, Inc.® Used by permission. All rights reserved worldwide.

Order additional copies from the author or on *Amazon.com*

restnow1418@gmail.com

gena@genabradford.com

genabradford.com

DEDICATION

When Jack proposed to me 51 years ago, I told him I couldn't marry him; I wasn't grown up yet. I was 20 years old, and he was 23. He then said, "Let's grow up together." That sounded reasonable—so we married. Little did we realize how much growing up we needed. But thanks be to God— where we fell short in immaturity and conditional love, God came through with grace and resurrection love.

I dedicate this book to you, Jack. You're the kindest man I know. You have laid down your life for me in servant love, taken care of me when I was in ill health, laughed at my antics, and believed in my dreams. I appreciate you. I could not have written this book or any book without your support, faithfulness, and prayers. I thank God for you, and for our wonderful children and grandchildren.

ACKNOWLEDGEMENTS

I praise and thank Father God, Jesus Christ His Son, and the Holy Spirit for redemptive love and grace. I was rescued from an orphan heart—a belief that I was responsible for everything—into a true abiding revelation that I am God's beloved child and in His full-time care. He is for us! We are His treasured inheritance. He sent Jesus to offer to all the abundant life, the opposite of burnout, and a revelation of our true identity. We can be forever grateful!

I believe that the most significant things in life are accomplished by a team effort and much prayer. This certainly is the case for the writing of this book. I thank those who've read the manuscript and commented, edited, and encouraged me: *Therese Marszalek, Sharon Hengy, Dr. Dennis Hensley, Karen Mains, Pastor Joe Wittwer, Patti Malott, Kathy Jingling, Kim Gardell, Laurie Klein, Jeni Stephens, Vanessa Shipowick, Lindsay Branting, Jeanne Feller, Kelly Ruffcorn*, my writers' group, and many more.

Thank you to my husband, Jack, for his patience and encouragement. Thank you to the men and women who read this book in the six-week group study at a local church. Their participation and faith in the message confirmed that it was indeed a relevant topic. It takes a team, a family, a host of prayer support, and much love to complete a book. God bless you all.

TABLE OF CONTENTS

Dedication .... *vii*

Acknowledgements .... *ix*

Personal Letter .... *xiii*

Day 1: *How and Where it All Began* 1

Day 2: *Let Me Take Care of You* 7

Day 3: *Black and White Thinking* 13

Day 4: *Being Responsive, Not Responsible* 17

Day 5: *Abba Chair* 23

Day 6: *Rest Is a Helium Balloon* 29

Day 7: *Flat Bottom* 35

Day 8: *Leap of Faith* 41

Day 9: *If It's Not Light, It's Not Right* 45

Day 10: *One Rotten Plank Sinks the Ship* 51

Day 11: *No Hats, No Costumes* 57

Day 12: *Some Pay to Climb Mountains* 63

Day 13: *Condemnation Fast* 67

Day 14: *The Only Way I Fail God* 71

Day 15: *He Loves Me; He Will Do the Most Loving Thing* 77

Day 16: *Don't Run Away; Run Deeper!* 83

Day 17: *The Cure for Regret* 87

Day 18: *Every Trial—An Opportunity* 93

Day 19: *A Pony—A Chariot* 99

Day 20: *The Un-pruned Tree* 105

Day 21: *"Just in Case" Thinking* 109

Day 22: *Permission to Get Well* 113

Day 23: *If I'm Willing, God Is Able* 119

Day 24: *I Have Time To Do the Will of God* 125

Day 25: *Thinking Paper Will Save Me* 131

Day 26: *Hurry Sickness* 137

Day 27: *Build a Sanctuary* 143

Day 28: *Rest on Every Side* 149

Day 29: *Traits of the Secure Child of God* 153

Day 30: *Refilling* 161

My Rest Confession 169

GOING DEEPER: *Questions for Reflection, Discussion, and Journaling* 171

Leader's Guide 195

NOTES 197

Recommended Reading 203

About the Author 205

PERSONAL LETTER

Are you tired? Have you been tired for a long time, but you keep pushing ahead because there's so much to do and people who need your help? You've been the responsible one—dependable. You feel you must do your part to make life safe and keep people happy. So, you work various jobs, you offer others food and encouragement, and you serve them in whatever way you feel they need. You stay vigilant, ready for action and ready to rescue. It all seems like the right thing to do; yet, you know in your heart you need rest. You realize you need to do a better job of taking care of yourself, but your needs and dreams always seem less important than those around you. You crave rest, but you don't know how to do it or even define it.

You might even ask yourself: *Why can't I rest? What is rest really?* Is it a vacation to an exotic island off the grid? That sounds dreamy. Surely, you could rest if no one could find you and you were on a beach far away from the cares of the world. But, where is such a beach? Who has the money to fly there, and what if your family, friend or job needs you while you're gone?

So, you stay home, keep working, taking care of others, and you ask yourself: *How do I rest at home, with all the needs of my family, the demands of work, and the world in crisis?* If you identify with this mindset, you may be on a path to burnout. Perhaps, you've already been there and keep finding yourself back on that familiar path.

This 30-day devotional book reveals heart-level beliefs about God and ourselves, beliefs that keep us tired. It is designed to share how those beliefs—which I call orphan thinking—can lead to burnout. The daily lessons are captured in personal experience stories and Biblical truths that radically change our view of our relationship to God, our Father. Each day has a theme, a revelation, scripture and words of wisdom, a *restercise* activity, and a closing prayer.

Burnout is not unique to women; men are vulnerable, as well. Although this book was originally written with women in mind, it can speak to men—as confirmed by the responses I've received. Sharing the daily devotional with your husband or a significant other can enhance the discussion and practical application. This book can be read by individuals or shared in a group setting.

Going deeper sections: There are additional questions for further reflection and journaling for individuals, couples, or group studies on page 171. Group studies may take six to eight weeks. Individuals set your own pace by listening to God's heart, absorbing all He wants to say to you, until you are ready to move on to the next day's encouragement and application. There is a leaders' guide at the back of the book for group studies.

God loves you with an everlasting love. He desires that all know His unconditional love on a heart level, not merely intellectually. I pray that God will speak personally to you and help you to come to the full knowledge of how deep, long, high, and wide His love is for you. You are precious to Him, and to this world. He demonstrated His love for us by giving us His Son Jesus—Who calls out to us daily, "Come all who are weary, and I will give you rest" (Matthew 11:28 NIV).

I invite you to share my journey to true heart rest and the recovery that awaits you and every child of God. May Christ Jesus fill you to the brim with life abundant and peace.

—*Gena Bradford:* a fellow traveler

MY STORY

The doctor's exam room had no windows and was exactly square, like a small prison cell. Her prescription, my sentence: "You must rest for at least six months. Every system in your body has been taxed to the point of burnout, clinical depression, caused by excessive and prolonged stress. There's only one cure, and that's for you to quit work, rest, and recover. I'll send you to stress management classes when you're more stable."

Now, I was not only sick, but terrified. At 53, I was too young to stop working or to retire. How would we pay our bills? What would my peers think of me quitting work to rest? Would I ever get my job back? I could not yet know that it would take three years to recover and I would never return to my full-time job.

Burnout could have been my middle name. Always over-doing, I felt responsible for everything and everyone. I viewed myself as a woman with many roles: mother, homeroom mother, scout leader, daycare provider, gourmet cook, teacher, wife, counselor, organizer, and "you can count on me" person.

A plaque on my wall read:

> *I am woman.*
> *I am invincible.*
> *I am tired.*

How tired was I? So tired that when I closed my eyes to pray, I would fall asleep; therefore, I prayed with my eyes open. Yet, at night I experienced insomnia. Daily tension headaches, heart palpitations, crying easily, forgetfulness, apathy for my job, persistent fatigue, digestion problems, and an inability to concentrate became normal. I became chronically ill from trying to hold my world together.

I once overheard a woman say, "Don't ask me to relax. It's my tension that's holding me together." It's funny, but sad. I identified with her, for I'd become adrenaline-driven, losing my way, even with lack of self-care. Many of us don't allow ourselves to rest, and we don't even know why. We've become addicted to a lifestyle that keeps us from knowing the truth that sets us free.

Our culture tells us that we should parent children, work hard and long at a paying job, and be "the hub of the wheel" at home. We are expected to keep life running smoothly for family and society. We feel obligated to volunteer at our children's schools, to take the kids to all their afterschool activities, to serve at church, to keep the home looking like a magazine spread, to cook healthy meals, and to be responsible for what seems like everything. And if this isn't enough pressure, family crises may add more. Sick children or aging parents may add care-taking to the list.

I didn't realize it at the time of my health collapse, but an even deeper root of expectation and performance had taken hold of my heart when I was 12 years old. My parents had divorced, and my dad left with his military assignment to live in Europe. I was the oldest child of alcoholic parents; I felt my safety depended on being strong for my mother and a protector for my younger sister. I believed I had to be brave, grateful, and responsible. I worked to fulfill the role of the good girl, the helper. I feared further abandonment. An orphan heart beat within my chest.

By the time I entered high school in Northern California, I vowed to earn good grades and many friends to compensate for my loneliness. I joined the leadership club, made the cheerleading squad, and tried out for plays. I finally felt of value when I'd been voted class president. But the next year of high school my mother moved us 400 miles to Los Angeles, away from the only place I felt accepted and safe.

The good news that came out of the move to L.A. was the Billy Graham Crusade. I attended, and when Billy told me (and all in the audience) that I had a heavenly Father Who loved me, I bolted to the altar to receive Christ as my personal Savior. It was such a precious gift that I continued to work for His love. I feared that if I didn't measure up to God's expectations of me, He, too, might walk away (like my dad had done), leaving me a spiritual orphan. I knew better according to Scripture, but it is said that we always fall back on our experiences until the truth reaches our hearts.

Truth comes by revelation, not information, and results in transformation. Truth is the gift that sets our hearts free from the lies that have taken root; it is the revelation that we are children of God—unconditionally loved, cherished, comforted, and provided for in every way.

In John 14:17-18, Christ said He wouldn't leave us as orphans, but would come to us and give us the Spirit of Truth, the Counselor, to be with us forever. Even when we love God and His Word, our deepest hearts may tell us that we are orphans. We begin to believe it, and live like it.

Perhaps, we don't realize we have an orphan heart. We only know that we're exhausted, and rest is not in our vocabulary. Here are a few traits and beliefs of orphan thinking:

1. People with orphan hearts don't know the unconditional love of God, so they feel they must prove their worth to others, to themselves, and to God. They work hard to the best of their ability, believe they must be brave and strong, without complaining. They believe that they won't be rejected or judged if they make themselves of value to others. Abandonment is their deepest fear. (Perfect love casts out fear.)

2. On a heart level, they expect life to be hard like a mountain to climb. So, they stay vigilant to stay safe, to rescue, and to be alert to problems.

3. They feel **responsible:** for making others happy and safe, pleasing everyone, keeping the peace, providing for others, and making something of themselves.

4. They fear suffering and loss, so they micromanage things. They live by to-do lists, adrenaline pushing, *caffeine,* and are always out of time. They feel they can never do enough or **be** enough. They over-commit. Self-care is their last priority.

5. They rarely allow themselves to play or rest. They're restless if they don't have a project. Being carefree isn't in their vocabulary.

6. They're not in touch with their deep feelings, because they feel they aren't important. They need to make others happy, but inside they're overwhelmed and depleted.

7. They love God and run after Him, trying to find Him. And at times, they run ahead of Him trying to fix things, just in case He doesn't show up.

8. They compare themselves to others and fear criticism. If they make a mistake they feel shame and embarrassment. They can't laugh at their mistakes.

9. They've experienced former rejection, abandonment, and conditional love.

10. They can't fathom or imagine how much God loves them. They only hope He does, because they have a hard time loving themselves. They feel flawed.

No worries if you identify with any part of this list, for it is my personal list of former orphan traits until God revealed and healed the lies and the vows of my heart. I worked hard to prove that I wasn't half-crazy or flawed, all the while believing that both must be true. I didn't know how much God loved me until I hit bottom. The author and singer, Sheila Walsh, now fully recovered from a nervous breakdown/burnout from trying to hold her world together declared, "I didn't know how close God lives to the floor."

The lies we have believed ring like cowbells echoing in a deep valley, especially when we feel we haven't done enough or been good enough. Vows to be strong and to make life safe must one day be **exposed, confessed**, and **released.** That is the redeeming work of the Holy Spirit—the Counselor and Spirit of Truth. Only God is strong and can keep us safe. And Jesus has declared us His spotless bride.

Are you ready to jettison fear of loss, abandonment and failure, feeling responsible for making life safe, people-pleasing, constant exhaustion, worry, and performing? Do you need a resting place? The Father's arms are open.

God was gracious in that He allowed my burnout in order to give me a new life, with new understanding, in a direction of health and wellness. My illness made me a ready listener, because I didn't want to go another mile in the wrong direction. **You can avoid burnout**! These 30-days of life-changing lessons and truths continue to bring me into a rested body and secure heart. I pray that they will encourage your heart to come into the rest that God offers us. Let us shed the orphan rags and put on His robe of righteousness purchased for us by His Son, Jesus, at Calvary. We are His beloved children. Nothing we can do will change that. Nothing we can do will earn it. When we accepted Christ into our hearts, we were introduced to God *as* our Father. Let's let Him father us!

It's time to get well, to realize your value and your true worth to God. You are His treasured inheritance. He will take care of you and your family.

My prayer is that each day you will find assurance that you are deeply loved by God, never to be left as an orphan, never to go through the depletion of burnout. If you have collapsed in burnout, like I did, I trust that you will find the strength and healing for the days ahead. Jesus has said that God the Father loves you as He loves Him. You are God's child—not an orphan (see Galatians 4:5-7). And as His children we may cry out, "Abba Father." You are cherished, never to be abandoned or alone. God is for you! All of heaven is for you. His rest awaits.

"For you did not receive a spirit that makes you a slave to fear, but you received the Spirit of sonship. And by Him we cry, 'Abba, Father'" (Romans 8:15 NIV).

—*Gena Bradford*,
April 7, 2019, Spokane, WA

HOW TIRED ARE YOU?

Checklist below. Count your points for every "Yes" answer.

- [ ] You are so tired that when you close your eyes for any reason, even to pray, you are in danger of falling asleep.
- [ ] You are a caretaker of someone: children, aging parents, adult children, a spouse or you do a job involving caretaking. (Some of you have to give yourself more than one point for this if you care-take in more than one area.)
- [ ] If you were a car, your gas tank would be on empty and you'd need an over-haul.
- [ ] You are always busy, on the run, hurrying to catch up, which you never can seem to do.
- [ ] You could say that you agree with the statement that there is never enough time to do what you think you should do, or what your boss or others think you should be doing.
- [ ] You forget to breathe deeply, and you don't know the definition of *free* time.
- [ ] You've even forgotten how to play. When it's time for a date with your spouse or significant other, you can't even think of one thing to do.
- [ ] You haven't read a book cover to cover in a month or year, or in your life-time.
- [ ] In the book of Hebrews chapter 4, when God said, "Strive to enter my rest," you got stuck in the strive part, and you don't have a clue about rest.
- [ ] You haven't taken a retreat from your responsibilities in over a year or more.
- [ ] You have many projects going and a to-do list as long as Santa's.

- ☐ Lately, you've found yourself singing or humming the song: *Nobody Knows the Trouble I've Seen*.
- ☐ You forget or don't take time to take care of yourself, because you are too busy checking off your to-do list. For example: you forget to take naps, get sunshine, exercise, take your vitamins, and do those things that nourish your body and soul.
- ☐ You've had a major stress or life change in the last year: a loss, a move, health issues, relationship difficulties, or a job change.

Scoring:

- 11-15 points: Call the ambulance; you are ready for resuscitation.
- 8-10: Get a wheelchair; your strength is gone.
- 3-7: Time to do some serious heart work. Hope this book helps.
- 0-2: Please write a book and tell us how you stay so rested in this frenzied world.

WHAT IS BURNOUT?

Simply put, burnout is physical and/or mental collapse caused by exhaustion, stress, or overwork. It is a state of complete depletion of energy and strength.

The list of symptoms can be both physical and emotional:

- Constant fatigue and exhaustion.
- Lack of motivation, initiative, or enthusiasm.
- Loss of creativity and efficiency.
- Poor sleep patterns and change in appetite.
- Confusion, forgetfulness, feeling detached.
- Everything, even a simple task, takes much longer to do.
- Feelings of being in survival mode and treading water.
- Inability to meet constant demands and feeling overwhelmed.
- Wishing you could flee, run away.
- Other physical symptoms may include headaches, back pain, muscle aches, gastrointestinal disorders, tight jaw, chest pains, and lowered immunity leading to frequent colds and sickness.
- Depression, anger, quick change in mood, less tolerance, and tears.
- A sense of failure, self-doubt, cynicism, helplessness, being trapped, anxiety, loneliness, listlessness.

Love Letter from the Father's Heart:

"My child, you are weary in much doing. I am with you, always close; even now My hand is upon your shoulder. Peace, beloved; be still! You have many cares. They are bundled upon your shoulders. Give the bundle to Me to carry.

"It is a season to grow. Cares and worries are like anchors that stop your forward movement. The river moves on, and you labor against the current with the anchor of fear, burden-bearing, and worry. Pull up the anchor! Give up the responsibility of feeling as though you must be the lighthouse watchman on stormy nights. I am the lighthouse. You reside in the boat without anchor. Let the wind of My Spirit carry you forward in My current.

"Decide to move forward. Know that I will sustain all the people you love. I will be their God and life. Go forward, beloved! My banner over you is love. I will guide you by the wind of My Spirit. Keep your eyes on Jesus, the author and perfecter of your faith. I am life, child, abundant life and joy."

Key Promise:

Jesus said, "I am going to the Father to prepare a place for you. I'll not leave you like an orphan. I'll never abandon you. In my name, the Father will send you another Counselor to be with you forever: The Helper, the Spirit of truth, the Comforter—the Holy Spirit. He will be in you and with you. He'll teach you all things and remind you of everything I have told you. I give you My peace, so don't let your heart be troubled or afraid" (adapted from John 14:2, 16-18, 26-27).

*30 Days
from
Burnout
to the
Heart of God*

DAY 1:
How and Where it All Began

My name could have been Harriet the Harried, Elizabeth the Enabler, Rita the Responsible, Martha the Micro-manager, Delta the Distracted, or "Oh—let me do it" Ophelia. Did I fail to mention that I'm in burnout, and my adrenal glands look like shriveled prunes?

This is my story. Perhaps you will laugh or cry, but my prayer is that as a result you will know your true name, the one God gives you, and how to become a person of rest.

I functioned quite well, I thought, with multiple titles as a mother of four children, wife, teacher, and Christian sister to all. I volunteered to lead everything, from homeroom mother to wellness committee chairman *(of all things)*. I made most of our meals from scratch, including homemade bread and soups. I even canned my own fruit, jam, and pickles every summer in my "spare" time: late at night or early in the morning while the kids were asleep.

I ran a daycare center in my home for 12 children, six days a week for 15 years. I returned to college at 36. While working, I finished a teaching degree. Then I worked another 15 years as a public-school teacher with special needs children. Every morning I pulled on the T-shirt with "RESPONSIBLE" written across the chest in big bold letters, for I was reared to feel responsible for everything and everyone. Perhaps every woman and man has such a T-shirt.

I was yoked with drivenness. The words *rest* and *play* were foreign to me. I ran on adrenaline until it ran out. With an empty tank, I faced what I most feared: the loss of my abilities to perform, to make life "safe," to provide income, and to fulfill my duties in the many roles I played. Surely, this would lead to rejection, disrespect, shame, financial ruin, and lack of purpose. How could anyone love me if I couldn't perform well and be an asset in even the smallest way?

It is said that breakdowns often lead to breakthroughs; death can lead to resurrection life. Look at the seed that falls into the ground and then blossoms to life in the spring. I needed to die to a performance-oriented life, and die I did to every name and title that once gave me pride and security.

In retrospect, I should have handed out party balloons at my own funeral—the death of my own expectations and strength—because through that death I would learn how to rest in Father God, faithful and strong, and discover His unconditional love.

My doctor was the first person I confided in, because I'd felt ill. Her diagnosis of burnout led me to a counselor. Together, their words confirmed that I could die if I didn't rest. They told me that burnout was an entryway to terminal illness if not corrected. Constant stress leads to debilitating disease. This drastic warning eventually gave me the courage to resign my job to save my life.

Restercise:

List all the "hats" you wear, all the things for which you feel responsible.

How tired are you?

Are you willing to hand the list over to Jesus and allow Him to take the burden, to lift the weight of those responsibilities? Give the hats to Him. Allow Him to reassign them, or give back to you only the ones that fit with ease. List the ones that fit well and are not burdensome.

He longs to make your way light. Ask Him to give you creative ideas on ways to share the load with helpers or to delegate the tasks to others.

Is everything you do necessary? Or, are you expecting too much of yourself?

Can you erase even one thing from your to-do list and replace it with free time for yourself? Start there, and ask others and God for help.

Prayer:

> Lord Jesus, forgive me, for I haven't known how to give You my every care and every sorrow. I'm still trying to be a good child by not complaining, by being brave and strong, by measuring up to the expectations of others, but my heart won't lie. I'm tired and hurting. I want to know You as the God of all comfort. I run into Your open arms for rest and peace, but first I give You the weighty backpack of cares, responsibilities, and the expectations of others and myself. I realize I have taken on this load to make life safe and others happy, as well as to give my life validation. I only need to please You, and You are not a harsh taskmaster. Help me see what is and isn't needed. You have accepted me as Your own dear child. In Jesus' name I pray.

Scripture Focus and Words of Wisdom

"Are you tired, burned out? Come to Me. Get away with Me, and you'll recover your life. I'll show you how to take a real rest. Walk with Me and work with Me. Watch how I do it. Learn the unforced rhythms of grace. I won't lay anything heavy or ill-fitting on you. Keep company with Me and you'll learn to live freely and lightly" (Matthew 11:28-30 *The Message*).

"Our souls are restless until they find their rest in Thee, O Lord."
—St. Augustine (354-430 AD)

"Much of our unrest emerges from misplaced trust; we rely upon our own strength to achieve what God intends. If I believe that I have to make it all happen, I'll never rest."
—Stacey S. Padrick, *Discipleship Journal* (Issue 127, 2002 p. 54)

DAY 2:
Let Me Take Care of You

With my resignation from full-time teaching came a dread that we would perish financially. I believed that I was just as responsible for our finances as my husband and that I should work to bring in as much income as possible to meet our family's needs and the desires I had for my children. I wanted to bless them and to help others. But, I didn't realize that I was trusting in myself, not in God. Fear drove my motivation to work. I feared failing God, my family, and others, so I performed. I was proud of my accomplishments; I felt needed and productive. My identity was in my performance.

But now, sick and unable to work, I not only feared this health crisis, but also what others would think of me: *She just couldn't measure up!* Embarrassed and ashamed, I wanted to avoid my peers. How would I explain to them my burnout? I didn't realize my pride was keeping me from their compassion.

My questions were many: *How serious is this? Will my spouse have a panic attack; will he hold up? Will we have to move and live in a cardboard box? Will my peers think I'm crazy for leaving a job at the height of my career? Will I ever work again? What if my children have financial needs and I can't do anything to help?*

Headed outside for a breath of air, I looked into the sky and told my Heavenly Father how scared I was. He spoke to my heart: "Let Me take complete care of you."

I cried, realizing that no one had ever taken complete care of me since I was a child. Just then, the memory resurfaced of the move to California at age 12, when Dad left and Mom said, "Gena, I need you to take care of your sister while I work nights." She had been a stay-at-home mom when married. "And you must keep the house clean and cook for the two male boarders I've rented rooms to, or we won't have enough money to live on. I'm counting on you." I remembered registering my sister on the first day of school every time we moved, as frequently as three times a year. Mom had trouble keeping up with the bills, couldn't pay the rent, or needed to relocate for the newest job. My heart felt old and responsible even then. I missed my pony, which was sold with the farm in Kansas. I cried at nights for my dad. I don't even remember him saying good-bye.

I lived up to Mom's expectations: be strong, responsible, grateful, and ready to do all that was asked of me for fear of more loss. I lived by that script for many years to come.

Now, after my burnout diagnosis, I was hearing my heavenly Father say that He wants to take "complete" care of me. I knew it must be God speaking, because I felt His love and all fear lifted. To this day, I remember the place I stood when He spoke to my heart, for I can never forget the times and places God speaks.

I cried with relief. I didn't know what it meant fully, but I knew that I was no longer to feel responsible for finances. I would obey my doctor's orders to rest, and I would reject all condemnation. I believed that God would prepare my husband and my family for the change.

A burden lifted that day, for my expectations of myself had been as heavy as a rock-filled backpack. Taking the burden off, I gave it to the Lord. I came home with a hope of getting to know God as provider.

The many years since that day have proven God faithful. When we needed a new roof, a man we had befriended surprised us with $5,000 in his will. It was just the amount we needed for the roof. We prospered, because we trusted and obeyed. I said, "Yes," to rest. God continues to teach me what rest looks like and what it's like to be His child.

Do you trust God with your finances? If you lost your job today, would you know in your heart that God would take care of you? If you have depended on your own strength, gifts, and abilities like I did, you may run aground with burnout. Even if the economy fails, God's economy never fails. He will never forsake you or leave you helpless. You can put your life, your family, and your job in His hands.

Is it possible that fear has been the motivation for your current job? Do you find this job depleting you? Perhaps God has a better plan for you. He knows what you're good at and what you'd love. He's a dream-maker, a dream-giver. If you are on a burnout path, if what you do brings you no joy but only fatigue, it may be time to hear from the Lord and take a leap of faith in a new direction. Pray about it, and seek professional or pastoral counsel. Ask the Lord to direct you to the right people, and He will confirm your path.

Restercise:

My journal became a place where I could write my prayers, thoughts, and insights while I was ill. It also became a place to listen to God. When asked, "Lord, is there anything You would like to say to me?" He would often assure me of His love or provide direction for the next step in my recovery. Journaling is therapeutic as you can access your heart by slowing down, sitting down, and writing. Find yourself a spiral notebook or bound journal, and spend time writing out your feelings, scripture promises, prayers, questions, revelations, and more. Talk to God, and wait for Him to answer. When we hear from God, we are forever changed. I call them life lessons.

Jesus said, "As the Father loves Me, so I love you. Now rest in My love" (John 15:9 NIV).

There are many journaling tools. Gather together in a basket or in your writing spot the following items: your journal, your favorite pen, colored pencils for sketching or underlining the revelations you receive in prayer, your Bible, a devotional, a separate to-do pad for annoying thoughts that want to side track you, a candle, favorite instrumental worship music to play quietly while you write, sticky notes, and pencil sharpener. You may think of more to add, like a cup of tea or coffee.

Create a quiet meeting place for writing your thoughts and sharing your heart with the Lord. Some people find a corner of their favorite coffee shop to write if there are too many distractions at home. Even 15 minutes of journaling can reveal what's on your heart and release tension. Years from now, you will look back on your journals and see how God has answered your prayers, and where you were with your heart at the time. It will bring joy to you to remember His faithfulness, and to see how you've grown.

Prayer:

Lord, You are my provider. If all my resources failed, You would still provide all my needs according to Your riches in glory by Christ Jesus (see Philippians 4:19). I'm sorry for all the times I've worried about finances. Fear has motivated me, not faith. Please forgive me, and guide me to the path of life. I'll look for Your direction each day. Your Word tells me that I can and will hear Your voice and that You will grant me wisdom if I ask. Thank You for loving me so much that You sent Your Son, Jesus, to grant me abundant life. I give all my financial cares to You, and I will give as You ask me to give, trusting in Your good care. In Jesus' name I pray.

Enjoy a version of the twenty-third Psalm from Japan:

The Lord is my pace setter … I shall not rush

He makes me stop for quiet intervals

He provides me with images of stillness which restore my serenity

He leads me in the way of efficiency through calmness of mind,
    and His guidance is peace

Even though I have a great many things to accomplish daily,

I will not fret, for his presence is here

His timelessness, His all importance will keep me in balance

He prepares refreshment and renewal in the midst of my activity
    by anointing my mind with His oils of tranquility

My cup of joyous energy overflows

Truly harmony and effectiveness shall be the fruits of my hours,
    for I shall walk in the pace of my Lord and dwell in His house forever.

Scripture Focus and Words of Wisdom

"Lack of trust is at the root of almost all our sins and all our weaknesses, and how shall we escape it but by looking to Him and observing His faithfulness. How many estimate difficulties in the light of their own resources, and thus attempt little and often fail in the attempt! All God's giants have been weak men who did great things for God because they reckoned (counted) on His being there with them."
—James Hudson Taylor (1832-1905)

"When life knocks you flat, roll over and look at the stars."
—Unknown

"I will never be shaken or fear bad news, for my heart is steadfast, always trusting in the Lord. My heart is secure without any fear, for in the end I will look in triumph over all that's come against me" (adapted from Psalm 112:6-8).

DAY 3:
Black and White Thinking

At first, when my doctor and counselor insisted that I quit work in order to recover my health, I kept going, pushing myself daily to just get by. But, then, even mentally, I was melting down: frequent tears, confusion, forgetfulness, depression, and an inability to make decisions. My visual perception was off such that I had two minor car accidents in one week, sideswiping a parked car, knocking off its mirror, and denting the bumper on another.

My anxiety about quitting work was so great that I sought counsel for weeks, in tears, needing much affirmation that resigning my job after 15 years wouldn't result in devastating losses. The first words of wisdom came when I was told that I had black and white thinking going on: I saw my job as life and safety (the white) and quitting that job as death and peril (the black). I attended a wellness workshop presented by Deanna Davis, Ph.D., author of *Living with Intention*. After sharing my fears with her, she replied, "You know, Gena, there are a lot of beautiful colors between black and white."

Those words brought vision to my heart as I realized that I hadn't left any room in my thinking for God—for all the multiple colors of things that He could do in and for me. It reminded me of the verse in 1 Peter 1:6 (KJV) where we are told that we will have "manifold" trials in this life. One definition of the word manifold means multi-colored. The Scripture goes on to say in 1 Peter 4:10 that we will also have "manifold" grace for every trial. I could see it: a perfect color of grace would match the same color of trial that I was going through or would face in the future. God could do things I never dreamed of to show me how to survive, and perhaps thrive. Encouraged, I decided to give up black and white thinking to discover the beautiful colors God would highlight throughout this season of my full dependency on Him.

I watched in awe as God stepped in to provide for our family, and invited me into His creativity. When I gave God the paintbrush, talents I'd never fully pursued began to emerge, and doors I'd never imagined opened. During the first few years of my recovery, I began to publish the many unfinished stories I'd packed away in boxes. I gathered songs I'd written and made my first recording of them. I was asked to do writing workshops, and I sang and spoke for events in the community. After months of rest, I worked part-time for the local university supervising student teachers. These activities brought me joy with no depletion. I still needed full rest days and didn't bring in my previous full-time job income, but my health returned, which is far more valuable than money.

The Lord knows how to provide for you. He knows the gifts He's given you and the plans He has for you. Jeremiah 29:11 declares that God has a hope and a future for you (without burnout).

Are you willing to give up black and white thinking to discover the beautiful colors He wants to paint upon your life, even the color of grace? Wise counsel is available to all who seek it, and the Holy Spirit, the ultimate counselor, is resident within every child of God. Don't hesitate to ask for His wisdom. Abundant joy and an array of colors await you. Count on it!

Restercise:

If you are good at foreboding and imagining the worst-case scenario, activate your faith, and replace it with the best-case scenario. Doing this when worry sets in will make God and you laugh with delight as you remember all things are possible with God. When you fear you're going under, say, "No, I'm going over... over to health and full provision, because Jesus loves me and I've given it all to Him. I'm resting in faith in His good heart toward me." Sketch or list the best-case scenarios for every problem you have. Then post it so you can say, "Amen!" every time you pass it.

Prayer:

Lord, I've been guilty of black and white thinking, forgetting how creative You are and how much You want to help me. Fear has kept me from taking the leap of faith to a better path for my life. I've felt responsible for holding my world together, when all along You were holding me and everyone I love. I'm embarrassed for thinking that I was keeping everyone safe by my efforts. I repent, Lord. I choose life. I choose to keep my eyes on You, even in the midst of my pain, my fears, and my recovery issues. Open my eyes to the colors of grace and opportunities You designed for me. I trust You with my life. I will obey Your leading. If You have a better plan for me and for my health, I want that and will pursue it. I love Your perfect will; it always produces life. Guide me, Lord. In Jesus' name I pray.

Scripture Focus and Words of Wisdom

"'I myself will help you," declares the Lord. O my soul, is not this enough? Do you need more strength than the omnipotence of the Trinity? Do you want more wisdom than exists in the Father, more love than displays itself in the Son, or more power than is manifest in the influences of the Spirit? Bring to Him your empty pitcher. Surely His well will fill it. Hasten, gather up your wants, and bring them here—your emptiness, your woes, your needs. Behold, this river of God is full for your supply; what can you desire beside? Go forth, my soul, in this your might. The Eternal God is your helper!"
—Charles Haddon Spurgeon (1834-1892)

"I am the vase of God; He fills me to the brim. He is the ocean deep; contained I am in Him."
—Angelus Silesius (1624-1677)

"We have this treasure in jars of clay to show that all this surpassing power and overflowing life of the living water of the Holy Spirit is from God and not from us. Inwardly we are being renewed, filled, day by day" (adapted from 2 Corinthians 4:7, 16).

DAY 4:
Being Responsive, Not Responsible

In the midst of burnout recovery, God spoke to my heart, declaring, "You are not responsible for everything and everyone; I AM! I just want you to be responsive to My love and leading."

Responsive, not responsible! That was a paradigm shift for me. I'd always felt responsible, except toward my own self-care. I didn't feel that I had a right to put myself first for any reason. I believed I was responsible for the happiness and safety of others, especially my family. So, I worked—I should say overworked.

That orphan feeling that I could never do enough pervaded my life, even when I became a parent. One Christmas morning, after all the abundant gifts were opened and my children were happily playing, I slipped into the bathroom and cried, because I felt I hadn't done enough for them; I wasn't enough.

Sadly, there are other examples. I never hesitated to buy my children the in-style clothes they wanted for school, yet I wore "high-water" pants years before they became popular. I worked as a daycare provider to pay for their music lessons, soccer, and dance classes, but never took a class for myself. My time out was a trip to the grocery store, where I'd spend a few minutes looking at magazines but never buying one, believing it was a frivolous expense.

The role of "responsible" followed me through all the years of child rearing, until I "crashed" physically, no longer able to be everyone's support system. How little I knew that I was trying to play God. I had forgotten that I was God's kid, and He wanted to take care of me.

This gift of burnout became a new building site for the Lord. He would lay a foundation of truth, line upon line, precept upon precept, as the Bible declares. He would manifest my true identity.

One of the first truths would be to exchange yokes with Jesus, who said that His yoke was easy and light. I affirmed on a heart level that He *was* and *is* the author of life. I repented of trying to be God. It was oppressively heavy to believe that I could actually save someone, or that I needed to save someone, in order to feel safe myself. I cried when I realized that I had not trusted in God's great love to meet all our needs.

It went even further for me, for I had another "responsibility" to turn over to the Lord—another opportunity to move to responsiveness to His Spirit. My mother, even after I became a mother myself, still wanted me to meet all of her needs and respond to her every desire. She expected me to call her daily, and if I didn't she'd get angry. She would tell me that it was my job to take care of her, a role she designed for me the day my father left her. Even though my mother was of sound mind and could work, she emotionally drained me by her neediness.

My counselor, during my burnout recovery time, gave me a visualization that helped me. She said, "I want you to see your mother coming down the street to your house, but before she arrives, Jesus is coming toward her. He puts His arm around her and turns her back toward her house. He is walking with her, and she is resting her head on His shoulder. He is meeting her needs. Now, you are free to do only what Jesus asks of you. You are to be led by love, not guilt, or fear, or obligation to someone's expectations of you. You needn't fear rejection, because God has you and your loved one. You are free to rest, recover, and get whole."

I took off the "I'm Responsible" T-shirt and put on the "I'm Responsive" one, so that I could be led by love, peace, and joy, not guilt or fear. If God initiates, then I'll have the passion, peace, and energy to follow through; I won't be doing life in my own strength or wisdom, or for the approval of others.

Now, I check in with Jesus before I say yes to anything, to see if I have His peace about it. There will be a joy in saying yes if He's in it. If there's heaviness, it's not my call. My relationship with my mother improved dramatically when I stopped trying to please her or gain her approval. Instead, I listened to the Lord. He would tell me when to call or drop in to see her. She became more appreciative and more reliant on the Lord herself.

Responsiveness is a world of difference from feeling responsible. It's gentle, and the Helper, the Holy Spirit, will enable us to do it.

I'm Responsible Traits

1. Makes life safe for everyone.
2. Makes everyone happy.
3. Performs well to earn love and acceptance.
4. Appears to never tire: runs on adrenaline (but you are tired).
5. Is brave at all times, even when sad.
6. Is good and helpful to avoid rejection.
7. Rescues and takes care of everything; is responsible.
8. There's no time to play; too much to do.
9. Puts self-care last and hides their dreams away.

I'm Responsive Traits

1. Gives responsibility for all back to original owner: God. Now co-creates.
2. Responsive to the Holy Spirit.
3. Rolls every care on the Lord.
4. Knows they are loved perfectly by God.
5. Doesn't try to measure up to others' expectations: free to be oneself, relaxed, cares, but doesn't carry.
6. Trusts God with their loved ones, and to be their provider.
7. Believes that God can redeem everything, even their mistakes.
8. Has no fear of failing God, and has no fear of abandonment.
9. Enjoys life: takes time for self-care, to play, to nap, and to see beauty.
10. Pulls their dreams out of the box and begins to live them. Creates again.

Restercise:

Are you ready to shed the "I'm Responsible" T-shirt and give it back to God? Let's ask Him to help us. Then, write down 10 things that you like doing now or loved doing as a kid. Pick one of them, and do it today. I took up bike riding again! Tree climbing seemed too perilous for my older bones. I also joined a tap grammas class.

If what you are doing is not bringing you joy, examine your motives for doing it.

_____

_____

_____

_____

_____

Prayer:

Precious Father God, forgive me for not fully trusting You. I'm sorry. I proclaim that You are Almighty God, and You only ask me to wait upon You, learn from You, and respond to Your leading. Help me to do what You've asked of me. I'm tired of feeling responsible for everything and everyone. I give you back the T-shirt. I only want to come into Your rest. Your Word tells me that those who wait upon You shall rise up with wings like an eagle, walk and not be weary, run and not faint (Isaiah 40:31). That's what I want. Teach me to wait, to listen, and I'll respond. In Jesus' name I pray.

Scripture Focus and Words of Wisdom

"In returning and rest you shall be saved; in quietness and confidence shall be your strength" (Isaiah 30:15 NKJ).

"The greatest burden we have to carry in life, the most difficult thing we have to manage is self—our emotions, our private weaknesses, concerns, worries, cares—all of which rob our joy. But in laying them down—lay down self. Hand over yourself and all your concerns into the care and keeping of your God, and leave them there. He made you; therefore, He surely understands you and knows how to manage you. Trust Him to do it."
—Catherine Jackson, *The Christian's Secret of a Happy Life for Today: Paraphrase of Hannah Whitall Smith's Classic* (1979)

"I have taken for my motto, '*not overwork, but overflow.*' Already it has made all the difference in my life. There is no effort in overflow."
—L.B. Cowman

DAY 5:
Abba Chair

The first prescription my doctor gave me for recovery from burnout was to take naps, as frequently as I needed them. I'd never napped; I used the time that my children were napping to clean house and catch up on my to-do list. After I started working full-time, naps were not an option. Even weekends were busy with errands and tasks. When my body felt tired, I just drank more caffeine and pushed beyond it, driven by my expectations of myself: super-mom, super-teacher, super-wife, *and super stupid.*

There was never a moment I wasn't thinking about what I needed to do next. So, with this advice to nap, I didn't know if I knew how or could relax enough to do it. But, burnout made it easy, for I was chronically exhausted. A soft, old brown recliner waited for me in my living room; I came to call it "my Abba Chair." Abba means "Daddy" in Aramaic (Biblical language), and I was learning how to let God be my daddy. I had no memory of resting in my dad's arms. He was absent or too busy to stop and hold me. Now, Father God, the creator of all things, made time for me to rest in His arms.

The first months of my recovery, I climbed into my Abba Chair three times a day to rest. I'd take no lists, no books or magazines, no phone, nothing in my hands. I was there to rest and receive. I kept a basket next to the chair with a soft blanket, cashmere warm socks (my feet are always cold), and a fleece eye cover to block light. When I laid the fleece cover over my eyes, I imagined that God's hand was upon my forehead encouraging me to relax, blessing me. I came not to do the talking with God, nor to pray and intercede for others; I came to receive His unconditional love, to listen, and to "just be" His child. When I climbed into that chair, I climbed into God's arms, and I stayed until I had the strength, His strength, to get up.

For months, napping was what I did most, with no apologies or defenses. It was a matter of an abundant life or death. The doctor explained that there's only one way back to health, and that is the path of rest and a change of heart on how I am to live this life.

My counselor called my husband, Jack, into her office to tell him what my needs would be in the coming months, maybe years. He agreed, though scared about the changes, especially the financial ones. I had brought in 60% of our income, and now that would be gone.

She assured him that God had made his shoulders broad and strong, and He would show Jack how to provide for our family for as long as it took for me to get well. We were uncertain if we would lose the house, but we resolved that it didn't matter where we lived, as long as we lived. Losing his wife to an illness—burnout can lead to catastrophic illnesses—wasn't an option.

So, when Jack came home and saw me in the Abba Chair, he was glad; he knew I was taking care of myself. There were many nights he fixed his own dinner after working all day, but I never heard a critical remark, only support and love. He had no expectations for me except that I get well.

Within the year, he received three promotions at work, adding $700.00 to his monthly income. We were able to refinance the house at a lower interest rate and have a more affordable monthly payment. God opened doors that kept us in our home and me resting. Jack realized, too, that his shoulders were broad enough to be our provision. He now proudly calls himself "Sugar Daddy." I always applaud when he does.

Abba Chair still waits for me, though it has been many years since burnout. I don't climb into it daily anymore, as my energy is full on most days, but when I am tired, I know where Abba's arms are waiting.

There's an anointing on that chair after the years of going there to receive God's love. I get my best sleep there, and I often get God's perspective on an issue.

Do you have an Abba Chair, or couch, or hammock, or backyard swing? Abba is waiting to hold you. He wants to give you rest. You're tired, and He knows it. The 23rd Psalm says that He would give us green pastures, still waters, and cause us to lie down in peace and rest.

Take only yourself, and give yourself unconditionally to God, who loves you unconditionally. Learn to know Him as the God of all comfort, as you discover your resting place.

Restercise:

Are you willing to give yourself permission to rest?

Will you clear a space?

    A favorite chair, the couch, your bed, or a blanket on the grass in your backyard can become Abba's arms. Nap or just rest your eyes 20 to 45 minutes, or more. If it's under an hour, it won't keep you awake at night, but it will increase your stamina. Try it today, and feel refreshed. Abba is waiting.

Prayer:

    Oh, Father God, to think that You wait for me, that You want to hold me and comfort me brings tears to my eyes. I am forever grateful, and I will not turn away from Your healing love. I give myself permission to slip away from the cares of this world into a resting place, to lay my head down as if upon Your chest, to listen to Your heart beat for me. I roll every care upon You, including the management of myself. Hold me. Kiss away my cares, Jesus. You are my Savior. I put the world in Your hands, all my loved ones. I come to rest and receive You and all You have for me today. In Jesus' name I pray.

Scripture Focus and Words of Wisdom

"Joy is the serious business of Heaven."
—C.S. Lewis

"True have His promises been; not one has failed. I want none beside Him. In life, He is my life, and in death He shall be the death of death; in poverty, Christ is my riches, in sickness, He makes my bed; in darkness, He is my star, and in brightness, He is my sun; He is the manna of the camp in the wilderness, and He shall be the new corn of the host when they come to Canaan. Jesus is to me all grace and no wrath, all truth and no falsehood; and of truth and grace, He is full, infinitely full."
—Charles Haddon Spurgeon (1834-1892)

"They travel lightly whom God's grace carries."
—Thomas á Kempis

DAY 6:
Rest Is a Helium Balloon

When the doctor said to rest, I honestly couldn't define it. My only visual image of rest was the week-long cruise in the Caribbean I took with my mother many years ago. When she was younger, she worked on cruise ships in the spa department and wanted to bless me with a vacation. And bless me it did. I left my husband, kids, the dogs, and the stress and snow of Spokane, WA, for the balmy weather of the Caribbean. For a week I played, swam with tropical fish, toured the islands, and sat in the sand without a care in the world. After all, who could reach me? I was 1,500 miles away without a cell phone.

Yet, even then I had my hand tightly gripped around my loved ones like they were helium balloons, fearful they would float away.

Two messages stood out for me on that cruise. One was a challenge from the Lord to let go of the balloons. I remember standing at the back of the ship as the golden light of sunset covered the horizon. *Let them come to Me.* I could see the Lord showing me that my fear of losing them had become like lead balloons to me, a heavy weight of responsibility. I wondered if I could do it? *Would I be all right if I let go? What if God took them all home to heaven away from me? Would I survive? Could God be trusted with what I love most?* I feel foolish for sharing this, because I know in my mind He can be trusted. But, my heart was holding on to those balloons, my children, like they were all who were keeping me safe and alive.

I held my fist in the air gripping imaginary strings of balloons, each representing a member of my family. And then, I let go. In my mind's eye I could see those helium balloons speeding toward heaven and the Lord's joy in my gift to Him. I honestly felt lighter myself; I danced my way back to my cabin, grinning because I knew in my heart that God had me and all that concerned me. I would be fine no matter what, because God held my loved ones and me securely in His hand.

Before the week had ended, I heard God's voice a second time. I was sitting on Grand Cayman's seven-mile beach, looking out into the clearest water I'd ever seen. It appeared that I could see into the ocean for miles. As the warm waters lapped around my legs, I thought: *I don't have a care in the world.*

And then I heard these words whispered to my heart: "I wish you were always like that." Could that be God, my Father, wanting me to be carefree? Is it even possible? Is it even right? I pondered that thought for days, wondering if I could give myself permission to be free of cares by casting all my cares upon Him (see 1 Peter 5:7).

I returned home rested and refreshed. That lasted maybe a week or two, for I was back to college, running my daycare center, feeling responsible for everything, and rearing my kids, two of the four with chronic health problems.

Yet, remembering what God said to me on that beach—that it was His desire that I be carefree with my heart at rest—I determined to begin a study of the definition of rest. I first checked the dictionary: "Rest is refreshment and ease, mental or emotional tranquility; freedom from worry or effort; relaxation and release from tension, and peace of mind."

No wonder I felt that I had to be so far away from all the responsibilities of home to be at rest. But, what does the Bible say about rest? Isaiah 28:12 declares, "To whom God says, 'This is the rest with which I cause the weary to rest. This is the refreshing,' yet they would not hear.'"

The word rest is from the early translation of *menuchah,* meaning "resting place, place of stillness, repose, consolation, peace, rest, a quiet place, and the condition of restfulness." It is derived from the word *nuach*, a verb meaning "to rest, soothe, settle down, comfort through the Lord."

Our Lord is the resting place for the weary. "He leads me beside the still waters of *menuchah*, the waters of quietness" (adapted from Psalm 23:2).

Now, after these years of recovery, I have come up with some definitions of my own:

Rest comes when I stop expecting myself always to succeed, to do it right. It comes when I learn to celebrate my failings, because I am willing to learn from my mistakes.

Rest is looking up at my Abba and seeing that He is looking at me, waiting for me to notice Him, to be fully present with Him, to enjoy Him.

Rest is the absence of fear. God has me and everything that concerns me.

Rest is knowing in my heart that I'm not an orphan; I'm eternally loved by God, and I'll never be left on my own, up to my own resources. I'll never be abandoned.

Rest is being filled with the Holy Spirit, responding to His love, and then walking in Spirit-led decisions. How do we get there? We pray, and we practice abiding in Him.

Restercise:

Are you holding onto and dragging lead balloons?

Would you enjoy, even for one day, not having a care in the world? What would you do, or where might you go, if you could truly play and release every care to the Lord?

What would true rest look like to you? Would you paint, build something, lie in the grass and look up at the clouds, take a recreational class, or buy yourself some flowers?

Bless the Lord today by choosing to give Him all your cares so that you may stay at heart-rest within the circumference of His arms. And then, go and play. When we recreate, we find our creativity and strength.

Prayer:

> Heavenly Father and Lord Jesus, save me fully from myself, from all fear and worry. Fill me with Your Spirit. I don't want to do life on my own. Come into my heart forever, and teach me how to live like a child of God, how to rest. May I live in the full revelation of Your abundant love. In Jesus' name I pray.

Scripture Focus and Words of Wisdom

"Great, many, and varied may be our trials, our afflictions, our difficulties, and yet there should be no anxiety under any circumstances, because we have a Father in Heaven who is almighty, who loves His children as He loves His only-begotten Son, and whose very joy and delight it is to support and help them at all times and under all circumstances."
—George Mueller, *The Life of Trust.*

"My soul finds rest in God alone; my hope and my salvation come from Him. He alone is my rock and my salvation; He is my fortress. I will not be shaken. My salvation and my honor depend on God. Trust in Him at all times; pour out your heart to Him, for God is our refuge" (adapted from Psalm 62:1, 7-8).

"When I don't trust the Holy Spirit, it's like jumping out of a canoe and swimming, using all my strength to make it to shore. When I do trust the Holy Spirit, it's like staying in the canoe and enjoying the scenery, while the Holy Spirit paddles right along with the current to the desired destination."
—Jeff Barker, a personal friend.

DAY 7:
Flat Bottom

My daughter, Hannah, hoped we'd buy her a backyard trampoline for her 15th birthday. She was a gymnast, so it was a perfect gift. After she left for college, it remained in the backyard like a tree house ... ready for someone to mount up, and in my case, to lie down on. I viewed it as a large, elevated hammock where I could gaze at the sky and rest. There, during the course of my questioning God about my health and seeking direction, He gave me a vision of a round-bottomed clay water pot with many handles. This pot had no stability; it rocked instead of resting, and while rocking it poured water in every direction. Anyone could take it by the handle and cause it to pour out.

The Lord said to my heart, "Like the pot, you've tipped yourself to the needs of everyone, never fully resting in Me, or allowing yourself to be filled to the overflow. I want you to have a flat bottom and from now on, to give only out of the overflow."

I laughed to think of the Lord telling me that I should have a flat bottom. A flat bottom is good, stable, and perhaps attractive. But, the thought of resting secure and allowing myself to fill up to the overflow was new to me. I thought I was supposed to serve others continually. But, here I was, in burnout, depleted and bone-dry. The doctor had just told me that my adrenals were shriveled like prunes from being overtaxed. This confirmed that neither my doctor nor my Jesus wanted me to be drained dry. They wanted me to be full of life, full of the Holy Spirit—the true Living Water. Jesus said that He came to give life and life abundant. To the woman at the well, He said that He'd give her living water so that she would never thirst (see John 4:10).

With this new vision of my life looking like a flat-bottomed clay pot with no handles, I pondered how it would look to give only out of the overflow. I could see that if I gave only from the overflow, I would never be dry or burned out. It could be effortless, because it would continuously flow over the top. The very life of God would give refreshment to others, and I would remain healthy.

What did I have to do? Learn to have a flat bottom, to rest in God and His provision for others and for me. Allow myself to fill up, nourish, and hydrate in all that God wanted to pour into me.

Wow! It felt as though God were giving me permission to be good to myself, to take a vacation from feeling responsible for everyone and everything. How would I do it? How would I not be captivated and held by someone's needs, wants, or expectations of me? I didn't know at first, but I learned to ask the Lord if it was His hand asking me to pour out, or if it was my fear that He wouldn't meet the needs of others or that I might disappoint someone.

Rest is a foundation of faith in the goodness and greatness of God. It's a belief that He alone is enough to meet each heart, and to save each soul in a multitude of creative ways.

I spent the next three years learning what it is that fills me up and what it is that drains me. I have given myself permission to be full and to refill as needed. I'm learning to play again, and I ask God before I say, "Yes," to someone's request. I nap, ride my bike and tap dance, have supportive friends, and so much more.

How full are you? Do you feel drained continually? Do you have many handles where you can be poured out? Burnout and drying out keep us from finishing the race God has set before us. We languish along the side of the path, in ill health or depression. As the old saying goes, "Slow and steady wins the race." Let's slow our pace to match the Master's. He walked, and He sat, and He rested. Let Jesus put His arm around your shoulder so you can lean upon Him and rest, giving Him the heavy load. You are His beloved. Let Him teach you how to rest.

All you have to do is say, "Yes!" to having a flat bottom.

Restercise:

Take time for friendships. Elizabeth Barret Browning once asked Charles Kingsley for the secret of his happy life. He replied simply, "I have a friend." Ecclesiastes (4:9-10) reaffirms that two are better than one, because they have a good reward for their labor. For if they fall, one will lift up their companion. Friendship gives us perspective, a shoulder to cry on, encouragement, wisdom, laughter, fellowship, and power in prayer. And, of course, don't forget your friendship with Jesus. Take time to talk to Him and listen.

Protect your soul-nurturing time, and give yourself permission to fill up. Call a friend for a lunch date or coffee/tea. Share your heart, listen, and pray together. You'll find wisdom, comfort, laughter, and support. You'll realize that two are better than one, and you'll be encouraged in those close relationships. Perhaps there is a weekly prayer gathering you can join? There is strength in numbers.

Prayer:

> Lord, I can't imagine how wonderful it would be to be full of living water overflowing to others without wearing me out or drying me out. What a beautiful picture of health. You want me full and at rest in You. It makes me feel like laughing, just thinking of myself splashing in a pool of water, refreshed and rested. Please help me, Lord, in my wellness journey. I've lost track of my self-care. But now, Lord, I see that it's Your desire for me to be healthy and rested, too. I'm your child; Your Word declares that You would lead me beside still waters and make me lie down in green pastures to restore my soul (Psalm 23:2-3 NKJ). I want that, too, Jesus. Today, I shall feed my soul and spirit, even if it's only for an hour. I can read the Bible, or take a nap, or call a dear friend. Lead me, Lord, in the path of life. In Jesus' name I pray.

Scripture Focus and Words of Wisdom

"It's a lot easier to serve when our cup runs over than when our batteries run out."
—Unknown

"My life is like a broken bowl, a broken bowl that cannot hold one drop of water for my soul or a warm drink in the searching cold; cast in the fire the perished thing. Melt and remold it till it be a royal cup for my King. Jesus, drink of me."
—Christina Rossetti (1830-1894)

"The fellowship of God is delightful beyond all telling. He communes with His redeemed ones in an easy, uninhibited fellowship that is restful and healing to the soul."
—A. W. Tozer (1897-1963)

"I am the vine; you are the branches. If you remain in Me and I in you, you will bear much fruit; apart from me you can do nothing" (John 15:5 NIV).

Love Letters from the Father's Heart:

"Child, I love you. My hand is upon your head. Draw close. It's not about your doing; be Mine, and do all in and with My strength. Let Me hold you and refill you. Add rest time to your daily list, and come and rest again. Don't forget the lessons I taught you when you first learned to trust Me.

"I want to minister to you, and I do that when you come to rest. I want to refill you, pour My life and love into you. Receive all the assurances that you are enough, even when at rest and especially when you are at rest in Me.

"Know this, My child, I'm enough to meet the needs of the whole world. You can afford the time to rest; you can't afford not to rest. Come lay your head upon My shoulder, and let Me support the weight of your cares. I love you without conditions.

"Just be Mine and enjoy Me. I'm fun, beloved. Commune with Me, and get to know Me. Hear Me laugh and sing. Even as birds sing with delight, I delight in you. When you give Me yourself, your time, I receive it as your gift to Me. I feel treasured and important to you. Come with tired body and empty hands, and I will fill you up with My love, My refreshment. Abba Chair is waiting for you."

Key Promise:

Jesus is able to keep me from stumbling and to present me faultless before His Glory, with exceeding joy! I'm called, sanctified, and preserved in Jesus Christ (see Jude 1:24, Jude 1:1).

DAY 8:
Leap of Faith

I knew I needed to quit work; I was just too afraid. To me it looked like cliff jumping. Whether I stayed on this side of the cliff with my job or jumped to resign, it still looked like death: death to my income and death to my physical body from ill health. What if I leapt to the other side, only to fall short of both cliffs? What horrible consequence would result in my fall? I believed I had no good choices.

As I prayed about it, I began to visualize these two steep cliffs, with me on one side looking at the other side, wondering if I even had the strength to jump. I took out colored pencils and drew the two ghastly cliffs, the steep gorge between them, and myself: a little stick figure standing on the edge trying to decide what to do. That was when the Lord opened my eyes to see it. He was standing in the gap of the gorge, bridging it, with His massive arms uplifted, calling out to me, "Jump, beloved! I'll catch you if you fall."

I threw my head back and laughed. "Oh, Jesus, You are delightful. I can see that this is going to be a win-win situation, whether I jump and land on the other side of the cliff or fall into Your protective arms. I can't lose!"

I shared the vision with a wise counselor, who said that sometimes we can't be 100% sure that the decision we're making is right, but if we're 70% sure, that's good enough. He also said that if I've prayed about it and trust the Lord to guide me on

Road X, but I was supposed to take Road Y, God is able to lift me from Road X to Road Y and get me back on track again.

I was 100% sure now that Jesus would catch me if I fell short. I desperately wanted to get well, and I was 70% sure that resigning was the right thing to do. In giving myself permission to leap, I quit my job at the top of the teaching pay scale, and I began the journey to wellness and learning how to rest in the Lord.

What cliff lies before you? What keeps you from making the leap? It helped me to draw Jesus in my picture standing between the cliffs: tall, strong, and loving, with His hands lifted up to catch me. I drew the conversation bubble with Jesus calling out to me, "Jump, beloved! I will catch you!"

Where are your crayons, colored pencils, or watercolors? You may have to take them out of the children's toy box and find a large piece of paper. I hadn't colored anything since childhood, but allowed myself to be God's child this day, carefree enough to draw. I posted my picture on the wall of my study to remind me that Jesus would catch me if I fell.

Where will you post your picture? You are the Lord's beloved; He has you in His hands, and nothing can take you out of His hands (see John 10:28).

Restercise:

Find a wise friend, pastor, doctor, or counselor to help you process your wellness journey. The decisions that need to be made and the concerns on your heart can be shared with safe people. My counselor once told me that nothing I could say to her would ever cause her to judge me. I needed to hear that, because I couldn't vent, cry, or share my fears and failures with someone who would judge me. I spent a year in therapy with a counselor who continually reflected God's love for me. I went in weekly to see her with a heavy heart and left with hope and a light step. A wise counselor can bring light into dark places and show us truths that can set us free. Everyone needs counsel at some time or another, even if it's from a best friend, someone who will love you no matter what. It can be humbling and scary to share our brokenness with another, but it can also be healing and life-changing. Who could you call or make an appointment with to begin the journey of sorting things out and sharing your heart? List a few possibilities. Ask others for references. Pray over them, and then call and connect. It made all the difference for me.

Prayer:

>Lord, is there a leap of faith I need to take to get healthy again, to learn to rest? Show me where You are in all of this, and guide me to wise counsel. I long to be whole, to be at heart rest and know how loved I am by You. Open my eyes to see and my ears to hear. Grant me a heart of understanding, and then I can turn away from the path of burnout to the path of life. I choose life and trust You will guide me. In Your precious name, Jesus, I pray.

Scripture Focus and Words of Wisdom

"Happy are those who know that discipleship simply means the life which springs from grace, and that grace simply means discipleship."
—Dietrich Bonhoeffer

"Plans fail for lack of counsel, but with many advisors plans succeed" (Proverbs 15:22 NIV).

"Did you receive the Spirit by observing the law (by works, by trying to be perfect) or by believing the Gospel? After beginning with the Spirit, are you now trying to attain your goal by human effort? Does God give you His Spirit and work miracles among you because you observe the law? It's because you believe and have been crucified with Christ, and Christ lives in you—living now by faith in the Son of God who loved you and gave Himself for you. Never set aside the grace of God, for if you could do life perfectly, in your own strength and wisdom, or by obeying the law, Christ died in vain" (adapted from Galatians 3:3, 2:20-21).

DAY 9:
If It's Not Light, It's Not Right

When struggling with a decision on whether to do something or not, my friend said, "If you don't feel light about it, something's not right." Jesus told us His yoke was easy; His burden was light (Matthew 11:30). When we are yoked to something heavy, we know it. It seems like pure drudgery, like walking up a steep hill.

My parents' divorce resulting in the absence of my dad, the constant moves from place-to-place with my mom's instability, and the burden of trying to hold life together for my sister and myself, left me with an expectation that life would always be hard. When I married and had my own young children, two with chronic health issues, stressful felt normal. If I wasn't under enough pressure already by being the mother of four, I continued to create even more by running a home daycare center that ran six days a week, twelve hours a day. Every minute was planned with something I was doing for others.

Then, I continued the home daycare part-time, while attending college to gain my teaching degree. I taught for 15 years before full burnout. The prescription for recovery required quitting all jobs, eliminating all stress in my life—to get well. It required looking at the expectations I had for myself and others' expectations of me. I spoke to God about it in one of my many rest sessions, and He spoke to my heart that His expectations of me were not harsh or long-listed. I could see that my personal to-do list was unending, and I was full of self-condemnation if I didn't complete it.

Those old orphan heart messages that said, *I'm not worth anything unless I accomplish "so much" each day*, drove me to near-death. Now, I was being led to examine my list, my relationships, and my tasks to see if they were light and right or dark and draining.

For example, a friend once asked me to join her in a ministry opportunity. Though it seemed good, I was learning to ask the Lord what He thought first. Jumping headlong into "good ideas" and feeling responsible for everything without being led by the Holy Spirit had resulted in my health crisis. So, I waited to give her an answer and instead asked the Lord in prayer.

I clearly heard Him say to my heart, "Don't yoke with unrest."

This curious remark prompted me to look further into her invitation. Had she asked God if He was calling her at this time to launch it? Had she waited on the Lord long enough, received her peace and strength from Him? I can't judge, for often my own heart deceives me.

Knowing it wasn't right for me, I declined her offer. If God wasn't in it, or the motive or timing was wrong for starting it, this ministry wouldn't prosper. That was exactly what happened; it eventually fizzled.

It's difficult to say "no" to friends or to good ideas, but it's harder to go through burnout and physical depression. I needed to stay on the track of God's perfect path of rest and wholeness for my life.

Now, when an opportunity arises to speak or minister, I check in with the Lord and with my body. I say, "Lord, what do You want?" I wait for His answer. And, when my body is tired, I rest. It had never occurred to me before to listen to my body. But now, if I sense a sinking feeling in my heart or gut, an uneasiness, I wait until I have peace to move forward.

What a relief to know that God's ways are pure, peaceable, and easy to receive (see James 3:17). When Jesus invites us to yoke with Him, He promises us that His yoke is light (and therefore right). Let's never forget that ease is better than *dis-ease*.

God loves you, and He invests the best in you because He knows He will get a glorious return on His investment. Give yourself permission to be blessed with the best, because you are His treasure, a gift to Him. He gives good gifts to His children.

Take a step in the direction of life, where every breath is easier. God will unfold the path before you. You take the first step, and He will be the solid ground beneath your feet. There are times the lightness of heart doesn't come until after we obey the Lord's leading in a particular area. A surrendered will to the perfect will of God always leads to peace, grace, and delightful surprises.

Restercise:

In your journal or on the next page, list all your daily and weekly commitments and activities. There are two columns: one for those that are light (a joy) and the other side for those that are heavy (a drain), or you could use two different colored highlight pens or pencils to distinguish the light and heavy activities. Then ask the Lord about the heavy side. Journal, listen, talk to the Lord, and see His perspective. Perhaps, it is only for a short season that you are doing this difficult task, and you can count on Him to give you strength because He's called you to it. But, if you are in an oppressive job, situation, or relationship, and you just don't know how to get out or make a change, this would be a good time to get wise counsel.

Learn not to "yoke" with unrest, and remember: "The Lord will guide you always; He will satisfy your needs in a sun-scorched land and will strengthen your frame. You will be like a well-watered garden, like a spring whose waters never fail" (Isaiah 58:11, Jeremiah 31:12 NIV).

Prayer:

> Lord, I need discernment on the activities or relationships that are wearing me out. Perhaps, I just need an attitude change or revelation to my heart of Your truth. Surely, I also need to build in time for rest and recreation. I'm willing and eager for You to show me what needs to change in my life, in my thinking. I want Your light yoke, Jesus. I receive it right now by faith, and I thank You that You have me and everything that concerns me. I trust You to teach me all things by Your Spirit. I commit my way to You. In Your precious name, I pray.

List all daily and weekly commitments and activities in the column that best describes how it makes you feel—either light or heavy.

LIGHT	HEAVY

Scripture Focus and Words of Wisdom

"God's commands are not burdensome, for everyone born of God overcomes the world. They who believe that Jesus is the Son of God overcome the world" (adapted from 1 John 5:3-5).

"Knowing God's perfect love for us casts out all fear" (adapted from 1 John 4:18).

"A perfect statement of humility is: 'I can't do it, God.' God desires us to be fully dependent on Him, because He can do it through us." Hudson Taylor, a Christian missionary to China for 51 years, wrote these words from God's heart:

> Bear not a single care thyself.
> One is too much for thee.
>
> Thy work is Mine and Mine alone.
> Thy work is to rest in Me.

DAY 10:
One Rotten Plank Sinks the Ship

Massive wooden ships have been around since the time of Noah. Sailing ships were used for war, transporting cargo, and exploration by many countries. Many have burned, but most have sunk because the flexing of wood while at sea causes the planks to twist and buckle. Then wood rot sets in.

A seaworthy ship could be expected to arrive at its destination, but one with a rotten plank could bog down with seawater and lie adrift, or worse, sink.

Our lives also may look good, seaworthy on the outside, but we might be completely unaware that there is a rotten, twisted plank in our soul. These planks are lies that we believe are true. One lie about our identity or a negative expectation can slow down, sidetrack, or even shipwreck our destiny.

For example, at age 12, I believed in my heart that I must have been unlovable or my father wouldn't have left me. This lie traveled deep in my soul, hidden below the surface. I'd grown up and received salvation through what Christ had accomplished on the cross; yet, I still wondered how God could really love me. I believed God accepted me because of what Christ had done, but did He like me? Was I lovable? Would He leave me if I messed up?

He exposed many rotten planks when I was laid up in dry dock for restoration, no longer at sea, too sick to work. God loved me enough to bring me into rest, repair, and truth, and to lay new, solid planks that would never twist or decay.

But first, God had to expose the lies I believed so that He could replace them with the truth that I *was* cherished. He looked forward to fellowship with me daily and would never leave me. The truth is that I couldn't sail to my full destiny without first knowing who I was to Him and in Him. I didn't realize what a treasure we are to God. We're His inheritance, His children. He is for us. All of Heaven is for us!

When I sank and could no longer work, I went to my doctors and counselor with the attitude: *Just pull me out of the water and see what the damage is.* But, the damage was more than physical. My beliefs and actions were sinking me: performing for love, feeling responsible (orphan thinking), and fearing rejection and loss. God had to fix that—and He did. He allowed me to lose my health in order to gain the truth of my worth to Him, my identity as His beloved child. Then He built me up again, seaworthy and moving toward my true calling and destiny.

I spent a year of recovery time with a Christian counselor who helped me see the underside of my soul. Every time I bared it, I cried because of the pain of those torn, twisted planks. But, eventually, God's truth and love poured through those gaping holes so I could sail again without fear.

If you feel bogged down in the water, like you're sinking, it's time to do your heart work. Jesus delights in us as a captain of a ship rejoices over his new charge. He wants to be at the helm of our lives, ensuring a healthy and successful journey. May God fulfill His dream and calling for each of us.

Help is waiting. It may be a doctor, counselor, pastor, friend, a recovery group, or all of the above. They are there to speak truth into your life and to minister to you. In the light of God's love and grace, lies and vows can be exposed, shed, and replaced with the truth that sets free. Reach out, and grab a hand. Once our heart work is addressed, we can sail on without fear, remembering that Jesus is in the boat despite upcoming storms. The destination and your destiny will be glorious.

Beloved, are you tired? Are you feeling burned out, treading water rather than making progress? I couldn't do it alone. I needed help, and I only wish I'd asked for it sooner, before my health failed. Let's ask our Heavenly Father to lead us back to port and into repair. He loves you; you are the apple of His eye. Come rest and seek wise counsel. Include the Holy Spirit, the Spirit of truth—the divine Counselor—in every decision, to orchestrate and guide the journey into wholeness. You are not alone.

Restercise:

One rotten plank can sink the most glorious ship. Child of God, ask the Lord if what you believe about yourself is true or a lie. Can you say that you know in your heart that God completely loves you? Have you made vows, promises to yourself, that were motivated by fear, judgment, lack of trust in God, negative expectations, or unforgiveness? Examples of vows made are how we promise ourselves to never show weakness, to fight our own battles, or to always be in control to avoid loss. These things can lead to shipwreck. Once a lie or vow is confessed to God, the truth becomes our banner, waving high like a ship's flag. Jesus is our strength! He loves us. He will fight for us and protect us. He is trustworthy.

We want to sail unhindered with Jesus, our ship's Captain. He's faithful to reveal what's in our hearts when we ask, "Search me, O God, and know my heart: test me and know my anxious thoughts; and see if there is any wicked or hurtful way in me, and lead me in the everlasting way" (Psalm 139:23-24 AMP). Then look for opportunities to do your heart work. Workshops, classes, mentoring opportunities, retreats, great books, and counseling are available for recovery work. The Holy Spirit will gently guide you. We all need healing. Take the first step, and sign up.

Prayer:

> Lord, look into my heart, and see if there is any hidden wound, resentment, or belief that will deter me from finishing Your call upon my life. I want to be an open book before You. I repent of _____.
>
> You are the author and finisher of my life. I want to be a healthy vessel carrying the fullness of You, Jesus, of Your Spirit in my life. You are my healer. I receive the truth that sets me free. I give myself to You and trust You to lead me. In Jesus' name I pray.

Scripture Focus and Words of Wisdom

"For even if the mountains walk away and the hills fall to pieces, My love won't walk away from you; My covenant of peace won't fall apart" (Isaiah 54:10 *The Message*).

"He is able to do immeasurably more than all we ask, imagine, or think according to His power at work within us" (adapted from Ephesians 3:20).

"Accustom yourself to the wonderful thought that God loves you with a tenderness, a generosity, and an intimacy which surpasses all your dreams. Give yourself up with joy to a loving confidence in God, and have courage to believe firmly that God's action towards you is a masterpiece of partiality and love. Rest tranquilly in this abiding conviction."
—Abbe Henri de Tourville (1842-1903)

DAY 11:
No Hats, No Costumes

It's been said that life is a stage and we all play various parts. I, however, had signed up for too many roles, with ill-fitting costumes and hats: fireman, consultant, fixer, homeroom mother *or should I say everyone's mother*, counselor, nutritionist, advisor, animal rescuer, volunteer *for everything*. When I was flat on my back from exhaustion, I saw the various costumes I'd been lugging around. Indeed, their weight had knocked me down.

Imagine the scene: I was onstage, performing in a large, dark theater. The spotlights on the stage kept the audience dark so that I didn't know who was out there, but nonetheless, I performed. Racks of costumes awaited my continual role changes. My favorite costume, and most used, was my fireman suit with hat, boots, and a wagon. Though it was too big and I could barely see from under the rim of the hat, I hauled the wagon across that stage, looking to save people and to put out fires in their lives.

I also loved the counselor and advisor hats. If you had a problem of any kind, I was compelled to offer my advice, provide the right answer to fix it, and make you happy. Making people happy was my ultimate goal, my role on stage; when a problem was solved and all were happy, I felt safe and needed.

The teachers loved me for appearing in September as a volunteer. I, of course, made the healthiest cookies and organized the parties. I attended PTO meetings, offering input. Field trips, special projects—whatever was needed, I'd be there. Every stray animal knew where I lived, and if you didn't have a place to go on Thanksgiving, my hostess hat and apron welcomed you.

I'm not saying that any of these activities are bad, but when you feel that you must play every role, you are a one-person show destined not for stardom, but burnout.

I could see myself stepping onto the stage, memorizing my lines, using great energy and pushing myself to prepare to perform each of my parts. I could see how confused and exhausted I was, trying to fit into the abundance of oversized costumes and hats.

Then came the God-inspired revelation. Looking out into the audience to see who was there, I found the room empty except for one person. There were no crowds of people judging my performance. I strained to see who was clapping, whistling, and cheering for me. It was Jesus! Now I could see that He and only He had been my greatest fan, the One who loved me unconditionally. Turning, I looked at the rack of costumes, hats, and talents I had used to gain validation.

"Beloved," Jesus asked, "are you quite done?"

"Yes!" I yelled with relief. Taking off the cumbersome hat and the weighty costume, I stood like a barefoot and carefree child, ready to be scooped up and taken outside to play. I noticed I was in my own clothes now. My white dress—I remembered Jesus had given it to me when I first met Him and asked Him to be the true love and Lord of my life. I had been dressed in His righteousness all along!

Skipping off the stage, I took His hand. We walked out of the dark theater, into the light of His world. His kingdom lay before us like a fruitful garden. I marveled at how light I felt just to be me, without a heavy, dark, oversized wardrobe. Joy and peace filled me as the sun showered my skin with warmth, my eyes now drinking in the beauty and colors of flowers and trees.

The One who mattered most loved me most. He wanted me free from performing for love—trying to do it all, to meet the needs of others in my own strength. Instead, I was to come into deeper relationship with Him, to know His love. He would begin to teach me to rest and to do all things from within the circumference of His arms, in His strength and anointing. I was God's own dear child, His delight and treasure, as are you.

Restercise:

What costumes do you wear that weigh you down?

_____

_____

_____

Others may have the giftings to do what you have found tiring. When I do what God created me to do, I feel joyful. It doesn't feel like a burden. It is just the right size, a gift motivated by love.

When I took on others' roles, it was a trust issue motivated by fear. Deep in my heart, I questioned. *Will God provide? Will He save those I love? Will we be safe?*

Take His hand, child of God. He offers rest. He offers no costume, but a robe of righteousness that covers you in His grace. Lean upon Him so He may kiss your brow and assure you of His constant love. Make a commitment to leave the stage of performance. He is always for you. Let Him take you to His garden, into the light of His love, by spending time in Bible study and prayer. Read Scripture as His love letter to you, and record it in your journal or on an index card. Those words of reassurance of His love and presence will breathe life into you throughout your day.

Prayer:

> Lord Jesus, I'm relieved that You don't expect me to save the world. I acknowledge that You have already done that by giving Your life for us on the cross.
>
> Show me the way out of darkness, confusion, and weariness. Lift off the heavy mantle of cares. I give you everyone I love and every concern. You alone are able to save the lost and heal the brokenhearted. I delight in the robe of righteousness You've purchased for me through

the cross. Its brilliant whiteness reflects Your beauty and gift of purity. I want to know the magnitude of Your love for me. Then, I will know true rest, play, and be enabled to fulfill the works You've created for me to do. Thank You, Jesus, for taking me into the light of Your love. I take Your hand. In Your precious name, Jesus, I pray.

Scripture Focus and Words of Wisdom

"God is more real to me than any thought or thing or person. I feel Him in the sunshine or rain; and all mingled with a delicious restfulness most nearly describes my feelings. I talk to Him as to a companion in prayer and praise, and our communion is delightful. He answers me again and again, often in words so clearly spoken that it seems my outer ear must have carried the tone, but generally in strong mental impressions. Usually a text of Scripture, unfolding some new view of Him and His love for me, and care for my safety... That He is mine and I am His never leaves me; it is an abiding joy. Without it, life would be a blank, a desert, a shoreless, trackless waste."

—William James (1842-1910)

"As a bridegroom rejoices over his bride, so will your God rejoice over you" (Isaiah 62:5 NIV).

"The Lord your God is with you; He is mighty to save. He takes great delight in you. He'll quiet you with His love and rejoice over you with singing" (Zephaniah 3:17 NIV).

DAY 12:
Some Pay to Climb Mountains

Jane and her friends were mountaineers. She'd save and spend several months of her salary to climb the highest mountains in the world. She considered that pure adventure. Though it took months of endurance training and expensive equipment, she saw mountain climbing as an opportunity to trust her guide and companions, to discover new things, and to see the world from its highest peaks.

I wasn't like Jane. I saw mountain climbing as a difficult, tedious, and nearly impossible feat, just like I saw the mountainous problems in my life: sick children, unpaid bills, and broken relationships. Worn out before I began, I believed all would be burdensome and hard to resolve. Funny, isn't it, how two people can see the same thing, a mountain, yet one is excited about the climb while the other is overwhelmed. That's when the Lord spoke to my heart about difficulties: "Some people pay to climb mountains."

I needed an attitude adjustment, a heart's belief that my Guide, Jesus Christ, would lead me to the top of my mountain and even carry my load, if I would trust Him to do it. An adventure in faith awaited me.

Rather than sighing, expecting the worst, and wearing myself out with worry before I even began, I could take the hand of the Master Guide and enjoy each step of the ascent by looking at Him and talking with Him. We would rest at the right spots, and occasionally I'd get to look back to see how far I'd come. I wouldn't want to look up to the dangerous peaks above, but would keep my eyes on the One Who loved me most and would never allow me to fall.

We can exhaust ourselves with worry and feelings of inadequacy. I always felt it was up to me to perform well, to do everything right. As a consequence, paralyzing procrastination would set in. I'd feel overwhelmed before taking the first step, and sometimes I'd go months with no steps at all for fear of making a mistake.

For example, for many years I was part of a worship team at church. Singing brought me great joy, and the group support took the weight of responsibility off of individual singers. One day, my family encouraged me to get my songs recorded as a legacy gift to my generations. God surprised me with the funding to produce my first CD, *Given Wings*, but I worried that I might make mistakes on a solo album, not do a good job, and shame myself. Fear set in! I didn't work on the CD for six months, until my dearest friend freed me with her advice. "Oh, this first project is just your practice CD," she said. "You'll learn by doing, and there will be more to come."

I went forward, giving myself permission to make mistakes, trusting in the guidance and love of God, Who was for me and would never fail me, even if I failed or missed a step. By His grace and enabling, the CD launched. I sang each song with joy.

Self-dependence, perfectionism, and performing for acceptance will keep us stuck at base camp, wishing we had someone or some way to get to the top of the mountain. As believers in Jesus, we can instead look at the mountain with a sense of adventure, believing that our guide will get us to the top, where the vistas will be well worth the climb. We'd take our first step and every step thereafter enjoying the journey with our constant companion, Jesus. He promised to give us His Holy Spirit, the Helper, who will never leave us somewhere on the mountain but be our guide forever.

Restercise:

Take out your journal or paper to identify what mountain lies before you today. What are you afraid to do? What are you afraid to lose? What seems impossible to resolve?

The Savior, your Guide, is prepared and ready to take you to the high places in God. You will get to know Him in the journey, and that, by itself, makes the journey most wonderful. Sketch the mountain, with you and your Guide climbing it together. He is carrying your load. Can you see it? This could be a grand adventure with a view from the high places. Sketch yourself at the top with a flag in hand to stake, declaring that through Christ all things are possible.

Keep your eyes on Him, and take the first step today in your mountain of adventure. Victory awaits you. Christ paid the price for your success at mountain climbing. Our part is to agree to move forward in faith, in His provision, strength, and love.

Prayer:

> Lord, give me courage to face my mountain. I've been afraid I would fail You, when all along You promised not to fail me. Let's do this together, step by step. I don't know how long it will take to reach the top, but with Your companionship and faith in me, I know we'll make it. Cheer me on when I'm afraid, and keep Your hand on my shoulder. I commit to a new attitude to see this mountain as a joyful adventure because I am with You. You will show me the treasures of Your kingdom. In Your name, Jesus, I pray.

Scripture Focus and Words of Wisdom

"His strength is perfect when our strength is gone;
He'll carry us when we can't carry on.
Raised in His power, the weak become strong.
His strength is perfect, His strength is perfect."
Song by Steven Curtis Chapman and Jerry Salley (©1988)

"By my definition, burnout is giving your energy to things not related to your life purpose. When you function in your purpose, you are like the burning bush before Moses. You burn brightly, but you are not consumed. You always seem to have the energy and will to do more."
—John Stanko, www.purposequest.com

"God has a resting place and an inheritance for me. He will give me rest from all my enemies around me so that I will live in safety" (adapted from Deuteronomy 12:8-10).

DAY 13:
Condemnation Fast

Do you find yourself measuring your days and even your self-worth by how much you accomplish in a day? My multiple to-do lists were endless: house chores and feeding the family; my job, community and church commitments; errands; and projects. When "very little" got done, I felt like I'd wasted the day. Self-condemnation and a driving taskmaster clamored in my head. I believed the lies: my value to God and others depended upon my being useful, helpful, and productive.

But now, in burnout, I had no to-do list. My goal was to survive another day. Still, regret badgered me: if only I could do more, help more, and be more available. I felt guilty watching my husband work all day just to come home to dishes and meal prep. My children carried the responsibilities of that first Christmas of my burnout by doing the shopping, cooking, and planning. I didn't have strength to buy even one gift for anyone. *Bad parent and lousy spouse* echoed in my mind.

As the season of Lent approached, a dear friend invited me to her prayer meeting. I accepted, knowing she had a couch I could lie down on. We prayed, sang, and worshiped God. She encouraged us to pray and ask God what He'd like us to fast from for one month. I immediately assumed He'd say chocolate or sweets, something I love. But instead, as I prayed and listened, He distinctly spoke to my heart: "I want you to fast from self-condemnation."

Whoa, surprise! I thought about how many times a day I judge myself for not measuring up, for not doing something I think I should be doing, or for doing a poor job. I wondered what it would be like never to criticize myself, or to be able to say, "Oh well, I'm okay and loved, even if I don't get anything done or do it wrong." What a novel idea!

Scripture tells us that there is no condemnation in Christ Jesus (see Romans 8:1). Could I fast from condemning myself? Could I turn a deaf ear to Satan's accusations?

I didn't realize how often I criticized myself until I was asked to give it up. Truly, I was delighted to give it a try and to keep the chocolate.

For one month, I blessed myself, whether or not I met any task. My expectations of myself were to be care-free. In fact, I had no expectations of myself except to take each day with joy. I didn't strive to measure up to anyone's expectations. I laughed when I forgot to go to an appointment. "Oh, well, it will all work out!" I declared.

I'm sorry to say that my perfect month didn't turn into years, but it did impact me. I remember my lesson that condemnation is not from the Lord, even self-condemnation. Paul said that he learned not to judge himself or be judged by others (see 1 Corinthians 4:3). Jesus said that He didn't come to judge this world but to save it (see John 12:47). So, who am I to judge what He has justified and declared righteous?

I repented. "Lord, I receive Your grace daily. If I ever accomplish a thing, it will be because You have enabled me. I am loved perfectly, not based on what I do but on who I am in relationship to You." Big sigh of relief!

Restercise:

Consider an experiment: a condemnation fast for a month. Listen, and notice your inner negative voice. How often does it speak? What does it say?

_____

_____

_____

Who does it sound like? Then, gently silence it. See if your joy isn't fuller, your step lighter, and all you accomplish a gift from God.

Prayer:

Lord Jesus, forgive me for judging and condemning myself when I didn't measure up to my own expectations. I can see I have been harder on myself than on anyone else. I've been tricked by the lie that my worth depends on my performance. I haven't lived in the daily grace and acceptance that You have provided for me. I commit to taking a condemnation fast. It seems wonderful to imagine a month without shaking my finger at myself. Could it be that for a month I could lift off all self-expectations and lay them at Your feet?

Wow, Lord, I joyfully accept Your offer to live without condemnation. Help me to discern the voices of accusation and judgment, and then to silence them by remembering that You didn't come to judge me, but to save me. Save me from myself, Lord, and teach me to be gracious with everyone, including myself. You are wonderful, Jesus! Thank You for all You have done and are doing in this world. I'm blessed because You love me. In Your name I pray, Jesus.

Scripture Focus and Words of Wisdom

"God fills me with His loving kindness and constant love each morning that I may sing for joy and be glad all my days" (adapted from Psalm 90:14).

"The pace of life and our preoccupation with unimportant things take so much of our attention. The significant things, like taking time to develop friendships, to read (the Bible) and pray, to read books that are challenging, to listen to God—these all get sacrificed on the altar of good works and Christian busyness."
—Luci Shaw

"Be at rest once more, my soul, for the Lord has been good to you. He has delivered my soul from death, my eyes from tears, my feet from stumbling, that I may walk before the Lord in the land of the living" (Psalm 116:7-9 NIV).

DAY 14:
The Only Way I Fail God

As a nervous child and a fearful adult, I took things too seriously. This fear kept me from doing things I loved, like singing in public. Though I'd been told I had a beautiful voice, I thought that if I missed a note or forgot a word, I'd die of humiliation. It wasn't until the Lord assured me that all of His kids could sing that I stopped comparing myself to other singers and found the courage to sing for public events.

This tension and fear of failure were part of my orphan heart, and they contributed to my body wearing out. When I could no longer work or do the things that made me feel safe or worthy, I discovered the truth that I could no more hold my world together than a child could run a city. My fears included thoughts like: *Will people still like me if I can't help them? Have I failed God?*

So, I asked Him, "Lord, have I failed You?"

His words to my spirit transformed my heart. "The only way you can fail Me is by not letting Me love you."

I pondered His response. It was as though I'd been holding an umbrella up between God and me, only taking it down to receive God's blessings when I felt I'd earned His love. Now, seeing that I no longer needed an umbrella, I realized the sun always shines God's favor, mercy, grace, and blessing upon those who love Him and will receive His love.

The revelation that I couldn't fail God if I loved Him and let Him love me, *especially when I felt like a failure*, brought me liberty. Now, when I sing, teach, speak, or even parent my children, I only ask that His grace and anointing cover me, that He be glorified. I invite His Spirit to sing through me, speak through me, to touch hearts with His love. And, when I sense His Spirit correcting me, it's always gentle, like a hand upon my shoulder showing me a better way. I quickly repent and receive grace.

We strive to please the Father, who already thinks we're wonderful, who created us, and would never consider throwing us away or abandoning us. The key? Stop expecting to be perfect! Only Christ is perfect. Let's commit our plans and our work to the Lord, and He'll direct our paths (adapted from Psalm 37:5).

In the coming months and years, I learned to depend fully on Him and to celebrate His grace covering my mistakes and failures. I learned humility instead of shame, gratitude instead of fear. God's Word assures us, "If we confess our sins, He is faithful and just to forgive us our sins and to cleanse us from all unrighteousness" (1 John 1:9 NKJ). "This righteousness from God comes through faith in Jesus Christ to all who believe" (Romans 3:22 NIV).

Grace covers us like Niagara Falls, pouring down upon those who desire God's blessing. Take down the umbrella and look into the face of God in Christ, for He loves you with an everlasting love.

Restercise:

Dare to be that child who believes in the good heart of God, that He is not a harsh taskmaster but a loving father.

Let's say, "Yes!" to being a receiver of the love of God in Christ Jesus, knowing that God accepts us at all times, even when we face criticism from others. We can make mistakes and remember that He can redeem them. If any mistakes or failures continue to bring you sorrow, offer them to the Lord to redeem. Some find it helpful to write them on paper and then burn it; others write them on rocks and throw them into the sea. Pray, and release them to God. The sins, mistakes, and regrets are forever gone once confessed. He remembers them no more; neither should we, except to be grateful for His forgiveness.

Now abide in His love. Find your resting place in Him, for there we bear fruit and good works, all in His strength and anointing.

Prayer:

> It brings joy and relief to my heart, Father God, that You don't keep a record of my sins and failures when I have repented. Lord, I repent of every way I have failed You or others. Thank You for grace and forgiveness. You never turn me away, even when I feel ashamed or worthless. You, Jesus, counted me worthy when You died for me while I was yet a sinner. Your Word tells me that You are for me, so who can be against me? I repent of judging myself so harshly, and I receive the love and grace You have for me today and every day. I take my umbrella down and look straight up to see Your smile. I receive Your Niagara Falls grace. Take me by the hand, Jesus. In Your name I pray.

Scripture Focus and Words of Wisdom

"The most effective workers I know are those who don't allow themselves a moment's anxiety about their work. They commit it all to Jesus, asking Him to guide them step by step and trusting Him implicitly to provide the wisdom and strength they need for each day's work. To see them you might almost think that they are too free from care, where such important matters are at stake. But when you have learned God's secret of trusting, you will see that a life yielded up to His working is one of rest as well as power."

—Catherine Jackson from *The Christian's Secret of a Happy Life for Today: A Paraphrase of Hannah Whitall Smith's Classic* (1979)

"Do you not know that you are the temple of God and the Spirit of God dwells in you?" (1 Corinthians 3:16 NKJ)

"It is impossible for a man to despair who remembers that his Helper is omnipotent."

—Jeremy Taylor (1613-1667)

Love Letters from the Father's Heart:

"Beloved child, I don't expect you to have it all together, to know it all, or do it all. You are My child. Children play and relax; they rest on their backs and look at the stars, or the trees, or the clouds going by. Children don't feel responsible for everything. They're free to enjoy life, the beauty all around them, the spontaneous moments. My joy brings strength and peace. I want you to be free to experience the abundant life I have for you in Jesus, My Son.

"You have time to do My will. My will is for you to enjoy Me, fellowship with Me, and see through My eyes. I want your joy to be full. Others will be drawn to Me by your joy and peace, for they are desperate for hope, to know that I am good, that I love them, and will be their Father, too. They will know that they are orphans no more. I will guide them. Rest in My love. Lay all before Me. I am your strength and song."

Key Promise:

The Sovereign Lord tells me to repent and rest, for in that is my salvation. In quietness and trust is my strength (see Isaiah 30:15).

DAY 15:
He Loves Me; He Will Do the Most Loving Thing

How do we rest when someone we love is suffering, or when we fear that someone will die? One of my adult daughters came close to death several times with both physical and emotional traumas. For years, our family never knew when the phone rang if we would be informed of her passing. This anxiety and worry wore me down and blanketed my heart. Indeed, like a wrecking ball, it knocked me off my foundation, further into burnout.

On Easter 1998, I sat in an arena with area churches gathered to worship. During the opening song, a soloist sang, "He loves me. He loves me. I can really say I know." The words pierced my heart, and I dropped to my knees in tears. *He loves me.* The revelation went deeper than my mind. It went into my spirit, my heart. *He loves me. He loves all I love. And, I can trust Him to do the most loving thing.*

That's when I released my fragile child into His love. I'd been holding on tight to the reins of her life in my every thought and constant prayer. Now, I could let go and trust the hands that lovingly created her and then took the nails upon the cross to save her. The clarity I had at that moment of God's deep and abiding love for me, for her, for all who love Him, washed away every fear of losing her. I rose to my feet free of worry. My daughter was secure in the arms of Jesus, who loved her perfectly.

The Lord did a miracle that day not only in my heart, but also in hers. He resurrected my daughter from her sick bed. That evening over dinner, we shared what

God had done and how He'd given her hope, strength, and a doctor's release from the hospital. A hospital chaplain had visited her the night before to tell of God's love and forgiveness. He read from Jeremiah 29:11, "God has a plan, a hope, and a good future for your life." The weight of oppressive fear was gone from both of us; Jesus would do the most loving thing. Whatever it was, I would accept it and trust.

Jesus loves you. He loves everyone you love. You can trust Him to do the most loving thing as you release your loved one into His care. We don't always understand why people suffer or why we don't see immediate miracles, but we can believe in the good heart of God and in all that Jesus has accomplished for us.

St. Augustine of Hippo (354-430 A.D.) said, "Understanding is the reward of faith. Therefore, seek not to understand that you may believe, but believe that you may understand." We can understand this: God loves us! That is enough in itself. If He loves us—and He does—then He also loves the people we love and cannot fail to perfect that which concerns them.

Our beloved daughter suffered many health trials, and as her parents, we suffered right along with her. I'd often throw myself into His arms and ask for His grace, comfort, and His perspective when she cried or was in pain. He is called the "God of all comfort." While you are awaiting your miracle, cast yourself upon His love; He sees and feels your tears. Allow Him to be your consolation until you get revelation. You are cherished by God.

A final word: if fear continues to assail you, if you hear a threat in your ear that your child is out of control and will suffer or die—run quickly to your Heavenly Father. This same daughter, as a teenager, was in grave danger with pain pill addiction, but all fear left when my husband and I placed her in God's hands, saying, "Lord, we fear for her life. Therefore, we surrender her to You, to Your complete care." Through tears we confessed, "If You take her home to be with You, we will praise You the same, whether she is with us for one day or 100 years. You, Lord, direct her steps, for she is fully Yours. In Jesus' name we pray."

Then when the accuser, Satan, tried to scare us by speaking into our ear that she was utterly lost and would surely die, we could tell him that he couldn't touch her, for we had given her to God, and she belonged to Him. We counted on God to do the most loving thing and then rested in that assurance.

"The Lord will perfect that which concerns us; Your mercy, O Lord, endures forever" (Psalm 138:8 NKJ).

Restercise:

List everyone who weighs heavily on your heart.

_____

_____

_____

_____

Now ask the Lord to do the most loving thing for them, for His perfect will, and for His glory. Thank Him that He has them in His hand, and that no enemy will be able to take them out of His hand (see John 10:28-29). Ask Him to send His guardian angels to watch over them, and then rest, knowing that God lovingly created us and cannot forget or forsake His children. Sing the timeless hymn *I Surrender All* ("All to Jesus I surrender; all to Him I freely give. I will ever love and trust Him, in His presence daily live") by Judson W. Van DeVenter.

Prayer:

> Lord Jesus, help me to remember that You are at work saving the lost and healing the sick. My part is to trust in Your love. I give You my loved ones. I trust Your good heart and ask You to do the most loving thing for them. Our times are in Your hand. You will comfort me when beloved family and friends go home to heaven. Until then, I ask You to keep them in Your care, grant them protection and grace, show them mercy, and forgive us of all our fears. Remind me, Holy Spirit, to surrender *all to Jesus*. Right now, I release all those I love and their needs to You. I will trust and obey. In Jesus' name I pray.

Scripture Focus and Words of Wisdom

"Can a mother forget her baby and have no compassion on the child she has borne? Though she may forget, I will not forget you! See, I have you engraved on the palms of My hands. You will never be ashamed, because you wait for Me, hope in Me, look for Me, and expect Me" (Isaiah 49:15, 23 *Amplified*).

"The promise of rest is offered to us today: let us attain it, a full and complete rest for the people of God" (adapted from Hebrews 4:1, 10).

"Fountain of life, and all-abounding grace, our source, our center, and our dwelling place!"
—Madame Jeanne Marie de La Mothe Guyon (1648-1717)

DAY 16:
Don't Run Away; Run Deeper!

King David in Psalms 55:6 declared, "Oh, that I had the wings of a dove! I would fly away and be at rest—I would flee far away and stay in the desert; I would hurry to my place of shelter far from the tempest and storm."

Many times, I wished I could flee stresses, conflicts, and the heart-wrenching pain of suffering. I imagined differently from King David; my escape would be warm and tropical… an island somewhere far from troubles, carefree. As the parent of four children, I had nowhere to flee and no money to flee with, so I cried out to the Lord for relief.

He spoke to my heart: "Don't run away, beloved. Run deeper into My arms."

When my daughter had to have a dreadful medical procedure, I felt frantic. I wanted to snatch her out of the hospital bed and run. I knew that wasn't an option, so I closed the door of her hospital room, pressed my nose to the wall, and cried out to Jesus to console me. Terrified of the danger of the procedure, I found His arms open and ready to comfort me with a depth of peace that no tropical island can match. He gave us both grace, and the procedure went well. This was the first of many times I would throw myself into a closet or behind a door to ask God for grace to endure her suffering, as well as for Him to comfort both of us.

He won't turn us away. He doesn't expect us to be brave or to "stuff" or medicate our pain. No, He wants us to share it with Him, to pour it all out so that He can pour His peace and perspective into us. I often ask Him to allow me to see the problem or person through His eyes. When He does, everything changes in my heart for good. His Word comforts me and reminds me that He has me, along with everything that concerns me.

I flee deeper into His arms when I am scared, in pain, worried, and just needing God to hold me. Sometimes I imagine that God has a pocket above His heart, and I am hiding in it. Knowing I'm there, every now and then He reaches to pat me, touching His heart and mine. In my 70 years of life, He has offered me shelter from every storm. I'm secure and at peace, because I've learned not to run away but to run deeper.

Are you willing to allow Him to be God of all comfort and wisdom? He is able and willing. Running away is only a temporary resolve, but running into the arms of Jesus is eternal life. Press in, dear one.

Stay, wait patiently... and see what God can do.

Just a note: there are times we must flee for safety if we are in an abusive relationship. We are guardians of our hearts and our children's safety. If the house is on fire, run out; equally, if a relationship is dangerous, evil, or abusive, get out. You are a treasure to God, and He has open arms and a plan for your protection. Call for help; there are safe houses and organizations available to help those in harm's way.

Restercise:

The God of all comfort is waiting to comfort you. He's ready to scoop you up into His arms as His own dear child. Run, beloved, into the arms of unconditional love and grace. Tell Abba all about it, and listen with your heart for His comfort. You can tell Him anything, for He already knows and has accepted you. Scripture tells us, "And this demonstrates God's love for us in that while we were yet sinners, Christ died for us. How much more shall He save us now that we have been reconciled through His life" (adapted from Romans 5:8-10).

Prayer:

Father God, You know the pain I'm in and the unfilled desires of my heart. I've felt like fleeing at times and have even sought false comforts. You know my disappointments and how long I've prayed for a breakthrough. I need Your *true* comfort, Your perspective, Your peace. I run into Your arms, trusting in Your love for me and for those I love. Comfort me, Father God. Fill me with Your Spirit, the Comforter. Open my eyes to Your wisdom, and grant me Your grace to endure all things with hope and peace.

Bring Your presence, Your Spirit, to my loved ones and lead us in the path of life, everlasting. In Jesus' name I pray.

Scripture Focus and Words of Wisdom

"God is the Creator and protector and the lover. For until I am substantially united to Him, I can never have perfect rest or true happiness, until, that is, I am so attached to Him that there can be no created thing between my God and me."
—Julian of Norwich

"Jesus said, 'Woman, where are your accusers? I don't condemn you, either. Go, and sin no more. I am the light of the world. Follow Me, and you'll have light to see and life. I haven't come to condemn the world but to save it'" (adapted from John 8:10-12, 12:47).

"We are human. We learn by trial and error. Failure is never ultimate or absolute. It is only a learning experience. The only real failure is the one from which we learn nothing. If and when we learn to laugh at ourselves, we shall never cease to be entertained!"
—John Powell

DAY 17:
The Cure for Regret

Regret is a downhill slide. Once you begin rehearsing your mistakes, your ride of regret picks up speed, hurtling you toward a crushing fear that your actions caused irreparable damage. You despair about the oppressive weight of responsibility for the consequences of your actions. You wonder if you'd been more loving or acted differently, could suffering have been averted?

For years, the voice of condemnation beat me into tears and shame. The "if onlys" traveled alongside. *If only I'd not hurt my child by what I said to her. If only I'd made a different decision. If only I'd waited. If only I'd gone. If only ...*

For me, regrets were packed into a large steamer trunk that was kept in the attic of my mind and heart. The enemy of my soul held the keys to accuse me, to open my sorrow once again, taking out each garment of shame and waving it before me. I, too, condemned myself because I was guilty. Though I'd asked the Lord and those I'd hurt for forgiveness, I just couldn't seem to forgive myself—to let it go. My mistakes and actions felt too grave; they'd caused suffering for myself and for those I loved. How, Lord, could I be free from shame and the sorrow I'd caused others?

"Leap off the slide quickly by remembering the cross," He answered.

The cross! Yes, I could see it; Jesus came to die for the sins of the *whole* world. That included me! The cross was big enough to reach from earth to heaven, to bridge the gap and cover my sins and the sins of the world.

I needed to embrace that cross, stand in its light, for it's a tower of salvation to all who look up and see it. I needed to declare when regret badgered me, "Lord, Your death upon the cross for my sins, for all the times I was unloving and hurtful, is more than enough to cover me."

As I proclaimed the power of the cross, all that Jesus had done for me, I opened the steamer trunk and threw in self-condemnation, remembering that Jesus is the Redeemer. I sealed the trunk with a fresh lock, threw away the key, and shoved the trunk down the stairs of my soul, out of my heart and mind, and obliterated it.

In my heart, celebration broke out with the proclamation of our Lord, "Behold, I make all things new!"

Christ can take a hill blackened with fire and turn it into a field of flowers. He can restore what was lost. He can create brand-new life, because we have become new creations in Him. What can't He redeem? What can't He hold in His hands and kiss to life again? He is the resurrection and the life.

Martha approached Jesus and said, "Jesus, if only You'd been here, my brother Lazarus wouldn't have died."

Jesus responded, "If only you would believe, you would see the glory of God" (see John 11:21-40). Jesus restored her brother to life, and he became a witness of the resurrection power of God.

Believe that God loves you so much that He sent His most precious gifts, His Son and His Spirit, to be with you forever. Jesus is the way maker; He is the One who makes all things new (see Revelation 21:5).

All we need to do is release the trunk of shame and receive instead the treasure chest of forgiveness and grace He offers us in its place. As we open it, we find His white robes of righteousness, our new garments.

Jesus spoke to my penitent heart: "Don't look back except to see how far you've come." I try to remember to keep my eyes forward on Christ, the author and finisher of my faith, my life coach. He waits at the finish line and cheers me on to keep going, trusting in Him and His love. I look ahead to the newness of what He has for me. Jesus, our Redeemer, is able and willing to forgive us and heal the hearts of all who seek Him.

Restercise:

Isn't it time to hand over the trunk of regrets by remembering the cross of Christ? He has a white robe with your name on it, along with all the treasures of your inheritance in Him. Do an exchange with your Savior: give Him your regrets—how you wish you'd done things better or differently, your disappointments in yourself and others, your sadness over the past. It may help to list them, and then draw a large cross over them to represent His covering grace and shed blood. He'll give you newness of life and His righteousness. Now you may burn the list, for your regrets and sins are remembered no more. Sing for joy! You are free.

Prayer:

My Lord Jesus, I believe You can make all things new. I rest in that. I shall keep before me the treasures You have given me: Your love and forgiveness, Your Spirit dwelling in my heart, and fellowship with You eternally. When condemnation comes, I'll remind the enemy of my soul that I am the beloved of God, forgiven and justified. I look forward to the new things You are doing in me, in my loved ones, and in all who trust in You. I believe You can and will redeem my mistakes and heal anyone I've hurt. I lift them now before You. In Jesus' name I pray. Amen.

Scripture Focus and Words of Wisdom

"Lord, I am a great sinner, but I have a great Savior."
—John Newton

"God does not treat us as our sins deserve or repay us according to our iniquities, for as high as the heavens are above the earth, so great is His love for those who fear *(revere)* Him; as far as the east is from the west, so far has He removed our transgressions from us. As a father has compassion on his children, so the Lord has compassion on those who fear Him" (Psalm 103:10-13 NIV).

"You want so much to heal yourself, fight your temptations, and stay in control. But you cannot do it yourself. You have to say yes fully to your powerlessness in order to let God heal you. Your willingness to experience your powerlessness already includes the beginning of surrender to God's acting in you ... your willingness to let go of your desire to control your life reveals a certain trust. The more you relinquish your stubborn need to maintain power, the more you get in touch with the One who has the power to heal and guide you. And the more you get in touch with that divine power, the easier it will be to confess to yourself and to others your basic powerlessness."
—Henri J. M. Nouwen, *The Inner Voice of Love*

DAY 18:
Every Trial—An Opportunity

When my children were still young, I read Hannah Whitall's book *The Christian's Secret of a Happy Life*, considered a Christian classic. Her chapter on what to do in the face of trials or emergencies still ministers to me today. She said that every problem is a potential steamroller. It can roll over you and crush you, or you can turn it into a chariot by climbing aboard, riding it, and staying above the problem. How do you climb up? Hannah says by using your wings of praise and thanksgiving to God. Stop in the middle—or better yet, at the beginning—of the crisis, and begin to thank God and praise Him for His help and faithfulness. Every trial is an opportunity to trust God and thereby bring Him glory.

Life offered me many opportunities to trust God. Certainly, I could see how little I trusted Him when it came to the welfare of my babies. Two of my four children had chronic health problems, and though I prayed, they were prayers of desperation. I inwardly feared losing them, because I'd experienced loss of my father as a child. My heart told me that losing a child would be unbearable, as I believed they were all I had. This belief made me vulnerable to great fear, which was like having a visible handle on my heart that any little crisis or lie from the enemy of my soul could shake.

Hannah Whitall's book helped me realize that I wasn't trusting God with my children. I named my third child after her because of her great faith. When my Hannah was two years old, she tumbled from the top of a wooden staircase to the landing below. As she lay stone still, eyes glazed and silent, a breathless proclamation escaped my lips, "Lord, thank You for an opportunity to trust You." My professions of faith didn't mean I wasn't afraid; it meant I would trust the Lord in spite of my fear.

I kneeled over Hannah, caressing her face, my tears streaming. I prayed, committing her into God's dear hands. Her eyes locked on mine, and soon she was up running again. I sat and cried with relief. Oh, the mercy of God in the school of life!

That beautiful daughter is 44 today, a mother to a six-year-old daughter and a ten-year-old son, both of whom love to climb. Will she cry out, "Lord, thank You for an opportunity to trust You!" when her child falls or faces a trial? I pray so.

To this day, I remember that I have a very present help in times of trouble. I don't need to stay hyper-vigilant. Hyper-vigilance leads to burnout. God has me and everything that concerns me. My job is to pray, to call others to pray, and to stand upon His word. Life has given me the opportunity to thank God hundreds of times as my children have faced crossroads, hospitalizations, and health issues. Each time, I realize I can choose to trust God or to go crazy with worry. Worry only makes me sick; trusting God brings rest.

I find heart rest by committing my cares to Him. I can't protect the world or my loved ones, but God can. I can't save them, but Jesus can. What a relief! I get to be God's child, not an orphan trying to make life safe.

Isaiah 54:13 has traveled with me all the years of motherhood, because it has reassured me of God's promise to parent my children as He has so faithfully parented me. May this scripture reassure you: "All your children will be taught by the Lord and great shall be the peace of your children" (NIV).

Restercise:

What are you guarding or worried about?

_____

_____

Why not use this as an opportunity to trust God and release your concerns to Him? Surrender your loved ones into His arms, committing them to Him, and be confident that the Lord is well able to keep and guard that which you've entrusted to Him until He comes (see 2 Timothy 1:12). When you do, it will bring Him glory because you've trusted Him. God will not drop that which you've committed to Him; He counts you and your loved ones as His treasure and inheritance.

A friend of mine created and decorated a little gift box; she puts the names of people and problems into it and then gives the gift to Jesus. She doesn't want to take back any gift she has given; therefore, it helps her to remember that all those concerns are now His. Be at peace. Abba knows your name and your address. You see … He lives in your heart.

Prayer:

> Lord Jesus, You trusted Your heavenly Father with everything and knew it would work together for good. Indeed it did, for You are the Savior of this world. I make the same decision now, to trust You that everything in my life will work together for good because I've been called according to Your purpose (see Romans 8:28), and You are still at work redeeming my life. May the first words out of my mouth in any crisis be words of faith and trust in You. You've given me wings of praise and thanksgiving; may I use them always. In Your name I pray.

Scripture Focus and Words of Wisdom

"Who is it that is your Shepherd? The Lord! Oh, my friends, what a wonderful announcement! The Lord God of heaven and earth, and Almighty Creator of all things, He who holds the universe in His hand as though it was a very little thing. He is your Shepherd, and has charged Himself with the care and keeping of you as a shepherd is charged with the care and keeping of his sheep. If your hearts could really take in this thought, you would never have a fear or a care again; for with such a Shepherd how could it be possible for you ever to want (lack) any good thing?"

Hannah Whitall Smith (1832-1911)

"Let not your heart be troubled, His tender word I hear,

And resting on His goodness I lose my doubt and fears:

Tho' by the path he leadeth, But one step I may see;

His eye is on the sparrow, And I know He watches me;

His eye is on the sparrow, And I know He watches me."

His Eye Is on the Sparrow By Civella D. Martin (1905)

Love Letters from the Father's Heart:

"Beloved, I will help you, with My mercy and compassion. I extend My hand to you. No obstacle shall keep you from going on with Me. You are up to the journey. All you need is a willing heart. I am your strength. You won't miss Me; you won't miss your calling. I am working in you to do My good pleasure. You will bear fruit.

"Right now, I am tenderly attending to you as a lovely planting, a tree in My garden. I am restoring your heart, hope, health, and strength. I am pruning, with your permission, sucker vines, and thoughts, and attitudes that drain you. I am watering you every moment, to keep you strong. I am keeping watch over you, lest anyone harm you. As oft as you would, come and drink of Me, the Water of Life. I am an oasis in the wilderness. Stay with Me, by still waters. Stay and rest! There is no hurry to push on. You have traveled far. Look back and see how far you've come. Our journey together has prepared you for the glories and joys ahead. Unload all your cares, fears, worries, the expectations of others, and of yourself. Take off all the weights that beset and make you weary. Give your cares to Me. Bask in My love and safety. Heal, beloved! Heal! I have you and all that concerns you in My care. Your part is to rest until you hear My voice say, 'Beloved, it's time to go together to love and feed My sheep.'

"Blessed and everlasting child of God, soak in the sunshine and summer rain. I will never leave you or forsake you. I am your healer. Fill up and rest."

Key Promise:

"You will keep in perfect peace the one whose mind is stayed on You and trusts You" (adapted from Isaiah 26:3).

DAY 19:
A Pony—A Chariot

The brightest moments of my childhood include the hours I spent on my pinto pony, meandering through cornfields and meadows, just the two of us. She, my chariot and companion, lifted me above the cares of this world. Adventure and comfort awaited me each summer morning as I climbed aboard her back to rest or to be transported to new vistas, thereby seeing God's creation from a higher view. There were no boundaries, no fences. This peaceful 5-acre Kansas farm was the last idyllic setting of my childhood.

Then tragedies, losses, and moves forced me to grow up and caused me to forget the innocence, playfulness, and freedom of childhood. I was twelve the day my pony was sold, because my parents were divorcing. My heart crashed as the new owner led my pony away, and Dad left for a job in Germany. Mom, my sister, and I moved to California to a rental house. She worked every night serving drinks at a bar, while I cooked for two male boarders, and took care of my younger sister. I'd become responsible!

We all carry sadness, and often, we carry people and their sadness. When the burden becomes too great, worry makes us old and tired.

Fear of more loss drove me to want to micromanage my life and the lives of my loved ones. If I could just keep them safe, help them choose what was best, I reasoned, all would be well.

We know that people, even our teen and adult children, must choose their own way; we can't choose for them. Still, we grieve when they are injured or make wrong choices and suffer as a result. I stopped living *my* life many times in order to try to carry someone who was in pain from wrong choices or from another's abuse. When I found others' pain unbearable, I cried out to the Lord.

That was when Jesus gave me a picture of me riding upon my childhood pony while He rode alongside on His horse. My pony symbolized comfort to me, and Jesus is my Savior and best friend.

He spoke to my heart. "Beloved," He said, "I have a pony for everyone who calls upon Me ... a chariot of comfort and grace, but each must have his or her own. You cannot carry them upon your pony. I will provide."

I saw that I could trust Christ to meet the needs of others as He was meeting my needs; He had a pony, my symbol of great comfort, for each person. Perhaps it wasn't a pony for the others, but a rowboat, a backyard rocking chair, or a puppy, but it was a tangible comfort, just right for each person's heart.

That revelation and the counsel of my pastor, Noel, who had lost his wife to cancer and reared his six children alone, enabled me to stand by my gravely ill daughter, Emily. She endured years of great physical and emotional suffering. At times it was more than I could bear; waves of sorrow crushed me such that I couldn't be in her presence without crying. I asked my pastor how he bore the pain. How had he kept from despair in front of his children and wife in her last days?

He said, "I asked God for grace."

"That's it?" I responded.

"Yes, and He gave it to me."

I cried at the thought of something so simple but powerful, to ask simply for God's grace to be with me and with those who were suffering. I prayed for God's grace to be with Emily and her pain. God granted me this gift, enabling me to remember that Jesus was with us. My heavy heart lifted into a smile in her presence. She felt my peace and God's grace—just what we both needed. "A merry heart does good, like medicine..." (Proverbs 17:22 NIV).

I have learned to repent of carrying the sorrows of others. *Care, but don't carry.* I've learned to pray, release, and remember that God can and will provide all that His loved ones need as they depend on Him.

Just as the precious blood of Jesus washes us from all sin, I sometimes ask the Lord to wash me from the burdens I am carrying. He faithfully answers that prayer, freeing me to enjoy His comfort, peace, and joy. I can continue with a light heart, knowing that my Savior is the Savior of the world, the God of every chariot.

Restercise:

Take time right now to list those who need God's grace. Don't forget to include yourself.

_____

_____

Ask Him to give you and those you've listed His grace and a picture of the chariot of comfort that He will provide for each one. Then go to them in peace, just to be present—a hand of comfort, a smile of reassurance that God loves them. He will perfect that which concerns them and will become their *and your* God of all comfort. You can teach them to pray by asking God for His grace and help in their time of need. His love is able to do more than we can ask or think.

(Scripture reference: Psalm 138:8, 2 Corinthians 1:3-5, Hebrews 4:16, Ephesians 3:20)

Prayer:

Father God, I ask for grace today to do Your will and to be Your servant in a hurting world. I also ask for grace for _____ as they come through this trial. May they see You, Jesus. May they know that you are near and that Your grace is sufficient for today. May they remember Your word and promise that You have spoken to them. Jesus, You said in John 16:33, that in this world there would be tribulation and trouble, but to be of good cheer, for You have overcome it. You promised to give us peace in the midst of the storm. I roll every care upon You and trust in Your good heart to work this all together for good. Bring healing and hope to us, Lord. In Your precious name, Jesus, I pray.

Scripture Focus and Words of Wisdom

"All works are in vain if they don't flow from grace. Fruit comes after the tree is well-rooted."
—Charles R. Swindoll

"Do you think, Christian, that you can measure the love of Christ? Think of what His love has brought you—justification, adoption, sanctification, eternal life! The riches of His goodness are unsearchable! Oh, the breadth of the love of Christ! Will such a love as this have half our hearts? Will Jesus' marvelous loving kindnesses and tender care meet with but faint response and tardy acknowledgment? Oh, my soul, tune your heart to a glad song of thanksgiving! Go through the day rejoicing, for you are no desolate wanderer but a beloved child, watched over, cared for, supplied and defended by your Lord."
—Charles Haddon Spurgeon (1834-1892)

"The Lord replied, 'My presence will go with you, and I will give you rest, because I'm pleased with you, and I know you by name'" (adapted from Exodus 33:14, 17).

DAY 20:
The Un-pruned Tree

Even now in my senior years, there are days I lose direction, feel pain and weariness in my aging body, and become overwhelmed with the complexities of life. But, I always come back to remembering a lesson I'd learned when my babies were toddlers. My husband's job moved our little family to another city and into a small rental house with a plum tree in the backyard. The tree had hundreds of small branches loaded with plums. I was thrilled. I could make jam!

After picking the fruit, I cut into them, only to discover that each tiny plum had a big pit. There were far more pits than pulp, and that batch of jam took hours to prepare.

"If your tree had been pruned to several main branches," a wise neighbor sympathized, "your plums would have been large and sweet. All those sucker branches drain the life from the fruit."

Sucker branches? That described my life! An orphan heart always overcommits and never wants to lose anything, even a sucker branch. I was an un-pruned tree, with countless branches trying to feed numerous projects while fulfilling the responsibilities of rearing a family and keeping a home. Even in my twenties, I felt tired and overwhelmed!

"Lord, I'm going in too many directions," I prayed. "I can't get it all done, and I don't know where to begin. Show me what's important to You. My life is bearing small fruit with big pits! Prune me, Father God."

"Feed your family and feed your spirit," He spoke to my heart.

I didn't know how all the other things would get done if I focused only on two main branches, but I obeyed. Daily, I began making prayer and Bible study a priority, along with menu planning and cooking nutritious meals. There were days I didn't get my house clean or finish my to-do list, but with a well-fed family and my heart resting in the love of God, it didn't seem to matter. Whatever I accomplished when I trusted in Him, became a gift of grace. New strength and peace blossomed. By abiding in His Word and giving Him all my cares in prayer, I found life tasted sweeter.

God wanted to nourish me in His love, and out of that fullness, I could nourish the ones I love. It seemed simple: feed and be fed.

Before ascending to the Father, Jesus asked Peter to feed His sheep. Feeding is important to God; we feed our spirit to be strong, and we feed others. When I don't ingest life-giving words from the Father, I am weakened, just as my body is weakened when I miss a meal. Jesus told us that we would bear much fruit, if we abide and rest in Him (see John 15:5).

Every day, we must first be fed in order to have the strength and the anointing to feed others. Our children and grandchildren, no matter their age, benefit from our words of life, our wisdom from lessons learned. There are days I barely ingest God's Word before I'm feeding it to a fearful or sick child or friend who needs assurance of God's love. God's Word never returns empty. It fills up our cup, no matter our age. Your encouragement from being with the Lord and listening to Him, is life-giving to others. Feed on Him, beloved of the Lord.

Restercise:

Sit down with Jesus, and feast on His love. He will strengthen you, but first He wants to hold you and reassure you that there is no condemnation with Him. He knows how overwhelmed you feel with many branches requiring much of you. The Bible tells us in John 15 that Jesus is the true vine, and our heavenly Father is the gardener. He will prune us if we're willing, but first He will show us what drains and what gives life. Take out your journal or a piece of paper and draw a sketch of yourself as a tree. How many branches are there? How many are essential? Are you willing to give the Master Gardener permission to cultivate your life and oversee your branches? He'll assure you that all is well that is given to Him.

Prayer:

Father God, I will take the time to feed my spirit in Your Word and in listening prayer. Thank You for the Bible, Your love letter to me. Feed me Your Word; open my understanding by Your Holy Spirit, that I may be taught and teach others. I give you my life and all its branches. I am willing to be pruned back to the vital branches, because I really do want to bear big fruit for the kingdom of God. Be my strength and my Gardener. Your Word says that I will bear fruit by abiding in your love. I choose to abide. In Jesus' precious name, I pray.

Scripture Focus and Words of Wisdom

"Grace and good works (that is, works done to earn favor with God) are mutually exclusive. We cannot stand, as it were, with one foot on grace and the other on our own merit."
—Jerry Bridges

"When we are kind to ourselves, we create a reservoir of compassion that we can extend to others. Our children learn how to be self-compassionate by watching us, and the people around us feel free to be authentic and connected."
—Brené Brown Ph.D.

"For it is by grace you have been saved, through faith—and this not from ourselves, it is the gift of God—not by works, so that no one can boast. For we are God's workmanship, created in Christ Jesus to do good works, which God prepared in advance for us to do" (Ephesians 2:8-10 NKJ).

DAY 21:
"Just in Case" Thinking

I'd rise early to hit neighborhood garage sales before seeking the Lord. I'd worry about how I was going to meet a physical or financial need. Soon, one garage sale would lead to another and then another, and half the day would be spent in search of a "treasure" or a good deal. I'd come home with things I didn't need just because it was a good deal. What if I or someone else really needed this toaster? Then, I'd have it to give. Being prepared is an orphan heart's motto. Living with a "what if" or a "just in case I need it" kept me bogged down with so much clutter that I couldn't find things even when I needed them.

The Lord asks me to trust Him in all things and with all needs. He asks me to have a "just in time" mentality, knowing that my God and Father will provide just in time. Psalm 34:10 states, "Those who seek the Lord shall not lack any good thing" (NKJ). It's also been said that God gives the best to those who leave the choice to Him. It's fear that gets me in trouble, the "just in case I need it someday" mentality.

I've learned that fear never produces good fruit or peace. The only way I can get rid of my garage sale addiction is to repent and remind myself that I am not an orphan. My Father provides all I need when I need it. I am free to give, to be generous, to be present with God and people. Perhaps, I am to stop at a garage sale to minister to the seller, to encourage someone, or to chat. My focus would be on the people, not the stuff. Now, that's true treasure!

It's not that I can't stop at a sale occasionally; it's just that I don't need to stop. I'm not compelled to do it for fear of missing something. That applies to store sales, too. I'd often charge something I thought would never be this low again, only to have a credit card debt that took months to repay with interest.

We are to be good stewards of our money, but a fear that I need to provide for myself is orphan thinking, and I am no longer an orphan. My Father is the King of Kings and abundantly capable of meeting my needs. I am learning to tell Him what I need, though He already knows, and to wait upon His timing and provision. I've discovered that while waiting, something I'd thought I had to have stopped seeming important. What a joy it is to give every care and need to the Lord—and what a joy to follow His leading and wait for His provision.

It's good to let others know our needs, too, especially if it's a big-ticket item, like a car. That way, they can pray alongside us, trusting the Lord with the answer. Sometimes He'll use people to help each other, like with my friend Sandi, who put her need for a car on the prayer list at church. Within the week, a couple had a car they didn't need any more as they were buying another. She received a free car at the right time for her need. God is like that. He loves us more than our earthly fathers or mothers do. He says that we know how to give good gifts to our children, but how much more we can trust the good heart of God to provide all our needs through the Holy Spirit (adapted from Luke 11:13).

My role is to ask with thanksgiving, then to rest in my Father's provision, trusting in His "just right" timing. Psalm 34:1 (NKJ) states, "I will bless the Lord at all times; His praise shall continually be in my mouth." If the door closes on something I longed to have or do—and it has at times—I can see, in retrospect, that even that was a blessing. God had a better plan.

Restercise:

We are not orphans; the Father, our Provider, has not forgotten us. He watches over each of us tenderly. Let's rest in that and have carefree hearts that can play, knowing that Father God is busy with what concerns us. Give your list of needs to God:

___

Then, find a way to play. Take out a board game, watch a funny movie, ride your bike, or do something else that will remind you that you are God's child, not an orphan.

Prayer:

Lord, You are my Father and Provider. Jesus, You are my Savior, and You do all things well. Forgive me for trying to provide for my loved ones and myself in my own strength and wisdom, instead of trusting in You. Forgive me for putting things before my time with You. Forgive me for being driven by fear and therefore missing opportunities to be present with You and Your people. Open my eyes to see and my ears to hear Your voice. I'll respond to Your leading and rest in the knowledge of Your first-class and timely provision. I choose to love You more than garage sales or earthly treasures. You are my first treasure. I find my joy in Your arms and in communing with You. I pray along with Your Word from Lamentations 3:21-26, "I have hope. Because of Your great love I am not consumed, for Your compassions never fail. They are new every morning; great is Your faithfulness. You, Lord, are my portion; therefore, I will wait for You. You are good to those whose hope is in You, to the one who seeks You; it is good to wait quietly for Your salvation." In Jesus' name I pray.

Scripture Focus and Words of Wisdom

"I have held many things in my hands, and I have lost them all; but whatever I have placed in God's hands, that I still possess."
—Martin Luther (1483-1546)

"Trust in the Lord, and do good; dwell in the land, and feed on His faithfulness. Delight yourself also in the Lord, and He shall give you the desires of your heart" (Psalm 37: 3-4 NKJ).

"And my God shall supply all your need according to His riches in glory by Christ Jesus" (Philippians 4:19 NKJ).

"They travel lightly whom God's grace carries."
—Thomas á Kempis (1379-1471)

DAY 22:
Permission to Get Well

Contributing to my journey of burnout were the chronic illnesses of two of my four children. Asthma, allergies, eczema, arthritis, and their emotional fallout from feeling flawed by illness were, at times, life-threatening. Terrified of losing them, I prayed, sought out doctors and naturopaths, and read and applied every bit of information I could find to save them. My orphan heart said it was up to me to rescue them, even though I knew I was woefully inadequate and fearful.

Over the years, I became sick with worry; suffering from ulcers, digestive disorders, and a lack of joy. I believed I could not be happy or well unless they were healed. My every prayer included beseeching God for their healing; I became so distraught that exhaustion set in, and I suffered a nervous breakdown.

My mother came to care for me and took me to a ministry meeting where a thousand women were worshiping God. Too weak to stand or even sit, I reclined on the floor just to soak in the worship. I began to join in the singing and praise, but still I begged God to heal my children.

"Lord, I love You. Heal my children." I repeated it over and over, until Jesus appeared in a vision above me. Dressed in a white robe, He filled the room with His presence. As I looked from His feet toward His head, I could see all of Him except His face, which was blotted out like a solar eclipse. In my confusion, I asked, "Why, Lord, can't I see You?"

"You love your children more than you love Me."

I was surprised, but I understood it and knew it was true! Since they'd been born, they'd been my first joy. My every thought was about them, their wellness, and how I could make life safe for them. I had put them before Him. My time in prayer wasn't to worship Him and be filled, content with His love. No, it was only in getting the relief I wanted from Him. Suddenly, I realized how idolatrous it was to put anything before my love for God, even my children. Yet, I felt I could not be happy unless they were happy, and I couldn't embrace wholeness for myself when they were suffering. It didn't seem right to be happy and healthy when they were sick. In my worry, I'd become sick.

I cry to think of it, except that our merciful Lord taught me so much. That day, on the floor, I repented of loving my children more than God. I told the Lord Jesus, "Whether You ever heal my children or not, I will praise You just the same. You are worthy to be loved and adored, even if they never get well. You are our Savior, and You have given Your very life for us. It is more than enough for me that You love me."

I then entered into true worship of my Lord with no begging, just a heart full of gratitude. Rising off the floor, I walked forward for prayer. I told the speaker about my children and my sin of worry. She gave me a word of knowledge from the Lord for my children about what to do next. And then, I went home healed, for within 24 hours, my strength, nerves, and peace were restored. It was a wonder to me how low to the ground I could feel one day, and how strong and lifted up I could feel the very next day from having been in the presence of the Lord. As I followed the word she gave, the Lord brought the next steps for my children's healing.

At another Christian conference three years later, I shared my daughter's ongoing health crisis with a minister, because worry had taken hold of my heart again. He said, "Our children are on loan from heaven." I wept with relief. I acknowledged we are all on loan from heaven, our true home.

Later that day as I sang in a large choir at the conference, the Lord spoke to my heart again: "Give yourself permission to get well."

"Yes," I said, remembering that Christ identified with and bore the sicknesses and sins of this world. He is enough, *more* than enough! He wants me to trust Him and to minister to others, especially my children, out of a full heart of joy, love, and peace. I'm to believe in His goodness and trust in His timing and His way of perfecting each of us.

My children are adults now, and I've seen many miracles since those days. There are more to come, but even if I don't see them completely healed on this side of heaven, I will praise Him the same as if I did. God is love, and I've learned He will do the most loving thing when I give every child and every care to Him.

Restercise:

Are worry and sadness eroding your health? Ask the Lord to show you if you have put something or someone before Him, and then repent. When we make our happiness dependent on a person, a job, or anything other than God, it has become an idol. Pray, releasing that loved one or thing into God's hands. Rest is giving yourself permission to be healthy in an unhealthy world. It is to identify with the Healer, not the sickness or the person. I encourage you to look for places to get prayer and ministry. Look for Christ-centered conferences or prayer meetings where there will be faith for healing or a chance for you to get a fresh revelation of the Word of God. We are the body of Christ, and we need each other just as a soldier needs other troops and commanding officers in battle. God will and can speak through our family in Christ to minister truth to our wounded hearts. Reach out when you need it. Ask and receive, that your joy may be full.

Prayer:

> Lord, if there is anything or anyone I love more than You, please show me, so that I may repent. My joy will no longer be dependent on my loved ones' health or well-being. I promise to praise You the same whether they are sick or well, with the same intensity and joy, as though they were completely healthy, for Your Word declares that You will perfect that which concerns them. My joy is in You, Christ Jesus. You are the Overcomer of every trial and tribulation. You have said in Your Word, "In this world you'll have tribulation; but be of good cheer, for I have overcome the world" (John 16:33 NKJ). I rest in that. I choose to be happy because You love me. I also give myself permission to get well, because You, Jesus, are carrying my loved one right now upon Your shoulders. Jesus, my Savior, I choose rest. In Your name, I pray.

Scripture Focus and Words of Wisdom

"What you can still do, while you are experiencing burnout, may be an indication of what your life purpose is. If you can paint, write, or play the piano when you're burned out, and those activities contribute to your healing, then there's a good possibility they are related to your life purpose. Burnout can be your friend, for it will help you focus on what it is that you were born to do."

—John Stanko, www.purposequest.com

Be Still My Soul
by Katharina von Schlegel (1697-1768)

Be still, my soul: the Lord is on thy side;
Bear patiently the cross of grief or pain;

Leave to thy God to order and provide;
In every change He faithful will remain.

Be still, my soul: thy best, thy heavenly Friend
thro' thorny ways leads to a joyful end.

Be still, my soul: thy God doth undertake
to guide the future as He has the past.

Thy hope, thy confidence let nothing shake;
All now mysterious shall be bright at last.

Be still, my soul: the winds still know His voice
who ruled them while He dwelt below.

DAY 23:
If I'm Willing, God Is Able

After all the years of longing for my father, I went to live with him when I was eighteen. Our first year together met a deep need in me to be known and loved by him. I cooked for him, and he was there to talk with me about my day, just my dad and I together at last. But, within the year, he remarried. Both his new wife and I wanted my father's attention, and it put a strain on their relationship. This spurred arguments and criticism.

Dad asked me to leave, and once again I felt abandoned. I gave up ever desiring a relationship with him. It was just too painful. I'd lost all hope of him ever being able or willing to father me, to love me. I believed I could never forgive him.

Four years passed without any contact with my father. In that time, I lived with a friend's family for a year, attended college, married, and gave birth to my first baby. My husband and I attended church every Sunday. One bright spring morning as we listened with our beautiful baby in our arms, our pastor preached on 1 Corinthians 13, the love chapter. When he said, "Love hopes all things and believes all things," conviction pierced my heart. All I could think of was my dad and how I had stopped hoping and believing for a relationship with him. It seemed too great a request. Why would God want me to forgive someone I feared would hurt me again?

But, that day, the truth of God's Word embedded itself into my heart like a barbed spur, and it wouldn't stop giving me pain. I asked my pastor to counsel me about my relationship with my father. Pastor Jake then told me something that has never left me. It brought me freedom not only in the area of forgiveness, but also in anything where I need God's help.

"God isn't concerned about your ability to forgive," he said. "He's only asking if you're *willing* to forgive, for He is able."

I hesitated, thinking of the door it might open. I couldn't bear the thought of being emotionally hurt again, but I knew that God was asking me to forgive. *I guess I'm willing to forgive,* I reasoned, *but I still don't want a relationship with my dad.* So I said, "Yes, I'm willing."

The miracle began. For three consecutive nights after dreaming that my father was suffering, I obeyed the leading of the Holy Spirit to call my father and tell him that I forgave him. Though I worried that my father might lash out at me, Jesus revealed to me that He would be my shield. One crucifixion was enough; Jesus carried that pain. He would stand between my dad and me as I kept my eyes on Him, trusting Him to catch the fiery darts of accusation. He would be my breastplate of protection. I was to remember my identity in Him. I reminded myself that I am God's child, loved and valued. Nothing will change that, not even an unkind word from another. What God says about me matters, not what the world or another might say. God's love never changes.

God also prepared my heart by filling it with compassion for my father, for when I forgave him, all anger left. As it turned out, my dad was so relieved that I had forgiven him that he showed up on my doorstep the next day with roses. From that day forward, we began a new relationship. I chose to remember only the good things Dad had done for me. God even gave me grace and appreciation for my stepmother. Jesus had forgiven and covered all of us when He'd died for us on Calvary.

Yes, forgiveness opened a good door to a restored relationship, whereby my dad accepted Christ as Savior and is now with Him in eternity. Had I been unwilling, my father would have carried the burden of guilt and perhaps not have surrendered his heart to Christ. I believe my grace freed him to receive God's grace.

The principle of being willing and thus depending on the Lord's ability works in all areas: self-care, finishing a project, going back to school to complete a degree, parenting, trusting God with finances, and learning to rest. The only ability we need in order for God to use us, is our availability.

My dad lived seven more years, and I cherish the memory of my time with him. I know I shall walk with my father in paradise someday. Both of us are orphans no more. Oh, the good talks we'll have then! I give all praise to Jesus, Who said to forgive and it will be forgiven of me. I thank Pastor Jake, who preached on love, and for the convicting power of the Holy Spirit, Who showed me how to love even when I'd given up hope. God is truly our ability!

Restercise:

In what area do you need God's ability? In forgiving someone, in self-care, or in overcoming depression?

We need God's help in countless ways. Thomas á Kempis, who lived in the 1400s, wrote, "Don't trust in your own knowledge, nor in the cleverness of any man living, but rather in the grace of God, Who aids the humble and humbles the proud."

When God asks you to do something or gives you a mission to accomplish, you may face fears, discouragement, or even mockers. Just say, "The God of heaven will give me success. Today, I will trust Him to protect my heart and to give me His anointing to do what He is asking me to do. I will take the first step, but He will make the ground solid under my feet. I am willing, Lord, to do Your will. Teach me, and give me Your grace."

Oswald Chambers declared, "It is quite true to say— 'I cannot live a holy life.' But you can decide to let Jesus Christ make you holy."

Prayer:

> Lord Jesus, I am encouraged to know that I am invited to live in Your strength, even when it comes to forgiving someone or completing a task. I am willing to forgive those who have hurt me *(name them)*, and I thank You that You are able to make it real in my heart. You will give me Your grace and love for those whose actions and words have caused me grief, even my enemies. You will be my protection and shield. You have said to pray for those who persecute me and to bless them (Matthew 5:44). I am willing in Your enabling. Precious Lord, in all areas of my life, be my strength and ability. Thank You for Your abiding presence in my life, through the Holy Spirit. In Jesus' name I pray.

Scripture Focus and Words of Wisdom

"Our faults are like a grain of sand beside the great mountain of the mercies of God."
—St. Jean Baptiste Marie Vianney (1786-1859)

"Lord, Forgive us our trespasses and sins, as we have forgiven others" (see Matthew 6:12). "Father, forgive them, for they do not know what they're doing" (Luke 23:34 NIV).

"To forgive heals the wound; to forget heals the scar."
—Unknown

"You gain strength, courage, and confidence by every experience in which you really stop to look fear in the face. You must do the thing you think you cannot do."
—Eleanor Roosevelt, *You Learn by Living*

DAY 24:
I Have Time To Do the Will of God

Stacks of paperwork clutter my desk at work. Housework, repair projects, the children's needs, and yard work stare at me. I'm convinced I don't have time to do all I think I should do, so I do nothing or the least important things, like fix myself a snack and read the morning paper.

I believe God has a plan for my day, but I don't know the plan. I worry that I'm not up to it, too distracted to figure it out, or unable to do it because I won't have enough time. I'm not always like this, but many days I am cluttered, confused, and tired by all that beckons to be done. I'm an over-scheduler; I think I can do more than I reasonably can do. When I do try to do it all, I fail or exhaust myself.

So, how do I decide what to do? Sometimes, I choose a good thing to do instead of the best thing, because I didn't take time to discern the perfect will of God.

I wonder what it would be like to do the will of the Father at all times. I wonder what "good" things I'd need to let go of, what events I'd miss, and what I'd have to deprive myself of. All of this thinking suggests that I don't trust the good heart of my Father to do what's best for me.

When I surrendered my life to Christ, I asked Him to have His way in me—and I meant it. I wanted Him to be Lord of my life. Paul the Apostle declared that it was no longer he who lived, but Christ who lived in him. Jesus declared that He only did what He saw the Father doing.

I'd like to live like that. Why don't I? Do I believe that God will deprive me of something I want? Do I feel responsible for everything and everyone? Am I willing to say no to self-comforts and instead to see what comfort and companionship the Father has for me? Am I willing to lay down my schedule for His, giving God my time, my day, and my life? Will I take time to listen to His desires for my day?

My answer for today is *YES!* I truly love the perfect will of God, because I know He loves me with an everlasting love. And, in the busyness of life, I get lonely for Him. In my distraction and doing, He gets lonely for me.

The revelation came to me one day: *I do have time to do the perfect will of God.* I don't have time to do everything I'd like to do, but God will generously give me the time and anointing to do what He desires for me to do. It's been said that multitasking robs us of being fully present with the one important thing we need to focus on. When we do what we are called to do, we are fully present, "in the zone" as some call it, losing track of time because we are fully engaged. Creativity, revelation, and joy are the result. I can experience that when I take a walk with my grandchild, when I have lunch and a heart-to-heart talk with a friend, when I write, or when I study God's word.

I must remind myself daily that I have all the time I need to do the will of God. If He wants me to call to encourage someone, I have time. If He wants me to write a letter or story, I have time. If He wants me to take a nap, I have time.

In her book *The Christian's Secret of a Happy Life*, Hannah Whitall Smith declared that she gave the management of her unmanageable self into the hands of God. I like that, because I can't manage my life with success. I can never measure up to my own expectations or to the expectations of others. How much better if I look to Jesus, Who loves me more than He loved His own life, and ask Him to direct my path, inspire my thoughts, grant me insight, and carry my load. What a privilege, not to have to prove ourselves to others or to God. He only asks that we love Him and respond to Him.

We can respond by laying down our lives into His hand. We struggle when we try to prove our significance by what we do. How much better it is to rest in the love of God, letting His love motivate us in all we do. We can trust in His grace, strength, and provision to accomplish His will. He's not a harsh taskmaster; He knows when we need rest and recreation, and He won't overburden us or wear us out. We do that to ourselves.

Restercise:

Let's come and refresh with the Lord of abundant life. Take some time to sit in the sun or in a quiet place and just be God's child with eyes and ears wide open, expectant to receive His love. Know that when He speaks a word to you, it will bring life, peace, and joy. Take the time, because God is the author of time and you'll have all the time you need to do the will of God. "The wisdom from above is pure, peaceable and easy to receive" (adapted from James 3:17). Then when you feel led by love to do something, call someone, pray for someone, or any other delightful thought—take the time to do it. You're on God's time. "Our times are in Your hand, O Lord" (adapted from Psalm 31:15).

Prayer:

Lord, today I take time to look up to heaven, remembering that You love me. I respond with gratitude. Father God, Lord Jesus, Your will be done in me today, as it is in heaven. I come to Your throne of grace with the desire to know You, to remember that I have time to do Your will, and to take joy in doing it. I wait for You and listen. You lead by love; therefore, I ask You to help me discern when I am being driven by fear, guilt, or some other flawed motive. Your Word tells us that Your sheep know Your voice. I only want to do what is pleasing to You and therefore healthy for me. You are the author of joy, peace, and rest. I receive all You have for me today: abundant life in Christ Jesus. Amen.

Scripture Focus and Words of Wisdom

"Let the beloved of the Lord rest secure in Him, for He shields them all day long, and the one the Lord loves rests between His shoulders" (Deuteronomy 33:12 NIV).

"Eliminate all things that cause negative stress. Live life as a child, with the spirit of play and fun and laughter. You'll live longer! Move where there is beauty, peace, and a place you can relax."
—Bernie Siegel, MD

"Live a sustainable pace; no cheating your family of time or cheating yourself of health, or cheating your Savior of fellowship time with Him."
—Andy Stanley

DAY 25:
Thinking Paper Will Save Me

For years, I've been complaining about my clutter problem. I collect things, especially paper: books and magazines of every genre, news clippings, and notes. I keep things because I think that these bits of information may save my life or the lives of my loved ones. Therefore, I have boxes full of clipped articles on health and medical research, home and gardening, things I hope to buy someday if ever I get the extra money, and how to organize my clutter. My garage and basement shelves are lined with books, boxes of teaching materials from teaching public school 11 years ago (in case I may need them someday), and countless other bits and scraps of paper, including thousands of recipes that I must prepare—only there's not enough years in my lifetime to cook all I've collected.

Because I have shelves and shelves of magazines, cookbooks, resource books, health books, and inspirational books, you'd think I'd stop buying more books. But, no; I have several subscriptions to magazines I love that are full of "information" I might need. I still take the newspaper, buy books at yard sales, and watch the news. I keep clipping articles and hoping that one of them will make my life better, even save my life or the life of someone I love.

I'm on information overload; I'm media crashing, confused instead of enlightened. And, I realize that I haven't believed in my heart that Jesus was enough. He saved me by His shed blood on the cross, gave me His Spirit of truth to live within me forever, and yet I've acted like an orphan, collecting bits of paper to surround me like a cocoon of perceived safety.

Instead, it's more like being buried alive in paper. My need is to trust that God will guide me moment by moment. His wisdom brings revelation, not just information, all at just the right time.

It's not that God can't use a good article or book to teach me, but I've made paper my security. I'm not a carefree child of God in that respect. I fear pitching my paper, which is a source of comfort and a stumbling block. I'm in too deep. I haven't known what to get rid of because the thought comes that I might need this book, article, or file.

The thought has occurred to me, *What if I threw it all out? Would Jesus be enough?* I think of a friend who lost her house to a fire. All her papers were gone. She said that in a way, it freed her. She knew that she was still whole and that God was her sufficiency. Now, she could travel light, go to the mission field or work abroad. She realized that possessions had constrained her.

Ah! I took a deep breath and marveled at the thought of how freeing that would be. Yet, I'd like to learn from her lesson and get free without the fire.

My paper clutter distracts and tires me. There's only so much time in a day, and I need to hear from Father God, to see what He wants me to do with my days, and to discern His plan for my life.

I determined to give my mind and heart rest by taking a one-week "information fast": no T.V., newspapers, Internet, books, magazines, or social media; it would be like years ago, when people lived off the land, even before radio. They lived in harmony with the day, the crops, the seasons, and listened to each other and to the Lord. A media fast, at least a partial one, would clear the clutter from my mind and help me to listen to the Lord.

I tried it. A friend offered her cabin at a lake with no phone, T.V., or Internet access. *Could I do it?* I wondered. The thought of being alone with the Lord without distraction thrilled me. I packed my bag and favorite foods and drove to the cabin by the lake. The quiet ministered to my body and soul. I walked in the beauty of the autumn leaves and spotted white-tailed deer passing by my window on the way to the lake. I wrote my prayers and thoughts in my journal and listened to the sounds of the birds. I napped and truly rested. Refreshed and encouraged at the week's end, I resolved to do it yearly.

I told a friend that if I gave away half of my belongings, I'd have twice as much room. I think it would be the same for my thought life. If I removed half of the media clutter I take in, I'd have twice as much time to listen to the Lord.

This year, I'm asking the Lord to help me clear the clutter so that I can better hear from Him, receive His wisdom and revelation for my life, and breathe.

I'm sorry that I've trusted in paper to save me. It seems ridiculous when I name it, but it had a hold on me. God will supply all I need just when I need it. That is my confession of trust in the One Who loves me most. I'm on my way out the door this week to collect boxes so I can carry paper out of the house to donate or burn. I've already posted an ad to donate teaching materials to new teachers.

Oh, I'm sure I'll keep some things, like favorite cookbooks, but what I keep I'll surely be able to find and share.

Restercise:

Frank Laubach wrote, "This year I have started out trying to live all my waking moments in conscious listening to the inner voice, asking without ceasing, 'What, Father, do you desire said? What, Father, do you desire done this minute?' My part is to live in this hour in continuous inner conversation with God and perfect responsiveness to His will, to make this hour gloriously rich. This seems to be all I need to think about."

Anything we use or do to keep ourselves safe instead of fully trusting the Lord to keep us securely in His hands needs to be put in its rightful place; we need to submit it to God. Wouldn't it be grand to travel light, knowing God is a ready resource, our wisdom and anointing for each day's needs? What's cluttering your thinking, and what would you like to be free from?

It may not be paper, but could it be a media addiction, food, T.V., or some other thing? Are you willing to take a step forward by confessing it to God and then getting His perspective and plan to be addiction-free?

Prayer:

> Lord, You are the wisdom I need, the path of life. You will not fail to help me when I cry out to You for knowledge. Your Word says that you give liberally to all who ask (James 1:5). I like that about You! You are my good Father, and I can ask for help whenever I need it, knowing that You will be there for me. Thank You, Father God. Thank You, Lord Jesus, and precious Holy Spirit, my Counselor. Guide me into all truth, and help me keep my path clear of clutter, stumbling blocks, or any addictions so that I may, as the apostle Paul described, finish the race You have set before me in good time. I ask this in Jesus' lovely name. Amen.

Scripture Focus and Words of Wisdom

"Being confident of this very thing, that He who has begun a good work in you will complete it until the day of Jesus Christ" (Philippians 1: 6 NKJ).

"The One who calls you is faithful, and He will do it" (1 Thessalonians 5:24 NIV).

"The Father loves you like He loves Jesus. Is this in your mind and heart as you come to prayer? You are not an orphan. You are not merely a 'servant' of God. You are a son or daughter. And with that comes privileges. 'But when the time had fully come, God sent His Son born of a woman, born under law, to redeem those under law, that we might receive the full right of sons' (Galatians 4:4-5)."

—John Eldredge

"May the God of peace strengthen, complete, and make me what I ought to be. May He equip me with everything good for doing His will, and may He work in me what is pleasing to Him, through Christ Jesus, to Whom be the glory forever" (adapted from Hebrews 13:20).

DAY 26:
Hurry Sickness

Phyllis J. Le Peau stated in her *Women of Rest Bible Study,* "Our busyness is a sin. In our rushing we reject God. His fourth commandment to us was one of rest."

I didn't know that hurry was a sin. Since I felt responsible for everything, it felt like good economy of time to fill every minute with a task. I left no margins or white space on the pages of my days. Therefore, at the end of the day, I was exhausted. I rushed from one unending to-do list to another. My sense of urgency even made it difficult to be wholly present with people. I found myself trying to hurry them along in conversation, finishing their sentences for them. I didn't give myself permission to rest while listening, to take time to hear what the Lord was saying or wanting to do through the conversation.

In John 11, Jesus didn't hurry; He tarried. When He received word that Lazarus was sick and dying, He waited. Lazarus had been in the tomb four days when Jesus came and called him back to life. He demonstrated that even death and time could not rule over Him, but He over them. He also revealed to Martha, Lazarus' sister, that if only she would believe, she would see the glory of God. And, she did when she saw her brother alive again!

In John 4, Jesus tarried at a well to bring a Samaritan woman to the knowledge of her brokenness, to the dryness of her soul. He took the time to tell her everything she'd ever done and offer her His grace, living water, and eternal life. In John 5, Jesus tarried at the Pool of Bethesda, speaking to a man who had been an invalid for 38 years. Jesus modeled heart-to-heart communication, being fully present, when He asked the man, "Do you want to be made whole?" The man gave the excuse that no one would help him. Jesus responded, "Get up! Pick up your mat, and walk."

Jesus stays at peace and focused by only doing what He sees the Father doing.

When I am truly present with others, I listen with my heart and God's heart, enjoying others and hearing their hearts. This creates a holy moment where the Holy Spirit brings light and healing to both of us. When I tarry, I allow time to see what God is doing. His tangible love can be expressed through people with a word, a hug, and compassion.

Tarrying leads to surprises like noticing how the sun reflects off the lake or the brilliant red of a rose. In God's handiwork, we are awed and see His signature. Every time we tarry, rest, and wait upon the Lord, Scripture tells us our strength will be renewed. Jesus encouraged His disciples to come away to a quiet place and rest—and He encourages us to do the same.

Father God doesn't have hurry sickness. It is written in Isaiah 30:18 that God *waits* and lifts Himself up, that He may have mercy on us. He waits for us to be ready to receive Him. The only place in Scripture that suggests God might run is when the father runs with open arms to meet his returning prodigal son.

Jesus gives the example of the good shepherd in Psalm 23, who offers rest, still waters, and green pastures to His sheep. He knows that if they feed and rest, their bodies will remain strong for the journey. We know as parents that feeding and resting our children, maintaining a balance between work and play, will be a recipe for them to thrive. Is our heavenly Father any less of a parent than we are? No! He is even more loving.

Hurry sickness leads to depletion; it stresses the body and its nervous system. The ears seem to go deaf. The heart pumps as if the body's in flight; the adrenals are overtaxed. The immune system gets fatigued, and illness sets in. Tired people are more prone to disease. Let me repeat that: dis-ease.

Perhaps one reason we hurry is because we feel responsible. We worry, *What would happen to me if I failed God or He didn't show up? What would happen if I wasn't hypervigilant, always ready to perform?* Our identity and sense of self-worth attach themselves to our doing; therefore, the more we accomplish the more valuable we feel.

Jesus said, "Don't worry or be afraid. Trust in Me and in the Father. I'll never leave you or ever forsake you" (adapted from John 14). *Walking* in the Spirit is called that because it is not *rushing* in the Spirit. We are led, not pushed. Jesus, our Good Shepherd, knows just the right pace for His sheep, never with any intent to weary us.

Restercise:

Let's ask the Holy Spirit to remind us whenever we are hurrying to repent and to remember His great love for us. Breathe, and let all cares go to God. As the prophet Isaiah said, "Those who wait upon the Lord, those who do not hurry, shall renew their strength." Rest is how our bodies and souls repair themselves.

When I find myself hurrying, sprinting ahead of Jesus, I'll try to stop, slow down, and check in with Him. I choose to remember that He loves me and I have time to heal.

Before you go to sleep tonight review your day as if you were watching a movie of yourself. What did you do and where did you go? Did you feel hurried? Who did you talk to? Did you take the time to listen, to be present, or were you impatient and feeling stressed? Try this practice for a few days. And then practice never being in a hurry by staying in communication with Jesus, and noticing what distracts you from that.

Cynthia Heald, the author of *Abiding in Christ*, says that anytime we sense anxiety, anger, or frustration controlling our behavior—or anytime we need grace, strength or wisdom, we may come to Him (even in the midst of activities/work) in the quietness of our hearts, share our burden with Him, and find rest for our souls.

Everything we do should be from a position of rest, abiding in the Vine Who is, by the way, not in a hurry. Jesus offers us His rest, abundant life.

Prayer:

> Lord Jesus, please put Your hand on my shoulder when I'm rushing or pushing again. I accept Your invitation to come into rest. I realize it's a trust issue, and I'm sorry. Lord, I want to walk in the Spirit, at Your pace. I want to play and rest. You are my Good Shepherd, and I will follow You and be present with You and with others. Thank You, Jesus, for loving me. I love You with all my heart. In Your name I pray.

Scripture Focus and Words of Wisdom

"God did not create hurry."
—Scandinavian Proverb

"A life of busyness drives us toward emptiness, but there is One Who fills us eternally."
—Denny Rydberg, author, speaker, and former president of Young Life.

"Beware of the barrenness of a busy life."
—Socrates

"I came to Jesus and drank, and I believe I will never be thirsty again. My life's motto has become 'Not overwork but overflow,' and it has already made all the difference in my life." There is no straining effort in an overflowing life, and it is quietly irresistible."
—L.B. Cowman

DAY 27:
Build a Sanctuary

When I was in survival mode—working full-time; going to school; and caring for my children, other people's children, my husband, and my home—I didn't garden or read for pleasure. All books had to be practical, like how to survive or cook for the family. I didn't paint, do crafts, ride bikes, or allow myself to do anything that would require me to be fully present and unrestrained by time. I admired people who did these things; I couldn't see how they had the time. Life felt like a state of emergency or at least like a machine that had to keep running, lest I lose all momentum and safety.

My friend, Laurie, planted a beautiful garden, painted, wrote songs and poetry, and decorated her home with cast-off garage sale items that she took the time to beautify into works of art. Going to her home was like visiting a retreat center—it fed my eyes and my soul while she nourished my heart with her gift of friendship.

When in burnout, daily resting, unable to work, and too tired to read, I reframed my thinking about my bare-bones existence. From my recliner I imagined a garden, a resting place. My yard was sparse and uninviting. I ignored it most of the time.

A whisper arose from my heart: *Build a garden.* Looking out at the backyard, I wondered, *How?* But, as the months went on, vision came as I studied other people's yards and flowers. I said to my husband, "Jack, let's build a garden."

His raised eyebrows clearly revealed his thoughts: *What will this cost me now, especially since we are on one income?*

I began to dream and pray. When a local home and garden show came to town, I walked through each display, taking notes. I asked neighbors questions about their flowers, what they were called, and how to care for them. Soon, they were donating starts from their plants: lavender, lilacs, lilies, peonies, daisies, and herbs. A neighbor gave me raspberry starts and promised that this very summer I would have sweet raspberries to enjoy daily. Jack caught the vision and helped by planting and watering. We found patio furniture at yard sales, and spray-painted the wicker white again.

Soon, my patio and yard looked like Eden. I sat outside in the spring and summer just to be alone with Jesus. I gazed at the sky, trees, and flowers, as I smelled the fragrance of lilacs and watched the hummingbirds and butterflies my flowers were attracting. Sometimes I'd take out my journal and Bible, to read Scripture and turn it into a written prayer. Most of the time, I'd relax in the glide rocker and rock to its rhythm, like a baby in the arms of a mother.

One day, I brought in cut flowers for my desk. A fragrant rose or a colorful Gerbera daisy reminded me of my heavenly Father's tender love; that He would take the time to create beauty for all people to enjoy.

I gathered my journal, colored pencils, a box of watercolor paints, and glide pens into a small basket. An art pad lay within reach, and I began to draw and paint pictures of the steps of faith and healing I was experiencing. I hung them on the wall to remind myself of all I was learning, like a first-grade teacher posting the early attempts of the students she wanted to encourage. Only, I was also the first-grade student learning about rest.

Soon, beauty blossomed in and around my home, accompanied by a spirit of rest. My friend Laurie noticed, and so did others. My home had become a sanctuary, a resting place for everyone who entered the door. Beauty is its own healing reward.

Restercise:

Dear one, perhaps you may feel that you don't have time or money to build yourself a garden or retreat area. You may have children in every room and clutter in every corner, but give yourself permission to find a place to come away and rest with Jesus. Perhaps it will only be a chair in a corner, but make it your chair for an hour. It has been recorded that the mother of the famous John Wesley had 19 children. She would sit in a chair and cover her head with an apron just to have time alone with Jesus. This was the only way she could keep from being distracted, but those prayers strengthened her and covered her children for the ministries that lay ahead.

Journaling is very helpful in this way. Write your feelings down; listen to what the Lord may be saying to you; sketch pictures of how sight (*the things we see*) turns into insight (*the spiritual lesson or application*). Record favorite Scriptures or quotes. It's your wellness journey, and it's precious—a legacy to share with others.

Every year, my garden grows more colorful and fruitful. Neighbors still share plants, and I add new features like stone pavers to extend the area for the BBQ and an eating area for friends and family. This year, I have four new strawberry plants. Every morning, I pick fresh berries for breakfast.

We are created in beauty, surrounded by beauty. Allow yourself to rest, create, and perhaps read a book cover to cover. Imagine that! It's okay to play. Playing frees our creativity. Roll every care upon Jesus, the One Who cares deeply and intimately for you, and then gather up art supplies and a journal, your children's crayons, paints, paper, whatever you have. Then express yourself. You will be delighted!

What will you allow yourself to do today or this week that brings rest and joy?

Prayer:

>Lord Jesus, teach me to rest. Remind me what it's like to be a carefree child with eyes to see Your beauty all around me. I give myself

permission to build a sanctuary, to play, to go on an adventure, and to dabble in the arts or to admire another's art. Perhaps I will even take a class in something where I use my hands to create beauty or make music. Inspire me by Your Holy Spirit. Lead me in the path of life. Forgive me for pushing myself too hard and forgetting to rest as You have commanded. I love You, and I love that You always have my best interest at heart. I rest in You, for You are my life. In Jesus' name I pray.

Scripture Focus and Words of Wisdom

"Is not the Lord your God with you? And has He not granted you rest on every side? Now devote your heart and soul to seeking the Lord your God, and begin to build that which He's called you to build" (1 Chronicles 22:18-19 NIV).

"This is that 'peace of God which passes all understanding,' that serenity of soul which it has not entered into the heart of a natural man to conceive. ... Waves and storms beat upon it, but they shake it not, for it is founded upon a rock. It keeps the hearts and minds of the children of God at all times and in all places. Whether they are in ease or in pain, in sickness or health, in abundance or want, they are happy in God."
—John Wesley

"Sometimes it's necessary to go a long distance out of the way in order to come back a short distance correctly."
—Edward Albee, in his play *Zoo Story*

DAY 28:
Rest on Every Side

In the midst of work stresses, fears about the health and welfare of my children, living paycheck to paycheck, and my own failing health, I cried out to the Lord for relief. We were in survival mode as a family, living day to day, trying to hang on like those in a rubber raft on a raging river. Life felt perilous at every turn.

King Asa's story, in 2 Chronicles 14, encouraged me when he said, "Let us build up these towns (of Judah). The land is still ours because we have sought the Lord our God; we sought Him, and He has given us rest on every side." So, they built and prospered.

This became my heart's cry, to have rest on every side. I wanted to build and prosper, yet we were in survival mode, daily engaged in spiritual warfare for our children, who were either ill or fighting addiction issues. Our marriage hung by a thread from the stress.

So, I studied to see how King Asa received this miracle as his enemies outnumbered his own army. "Then Asa called to the Lord his God and said, 'Lord, there is no one like You to help the powerless against the mighty. Help us, O Lord our God, for we rely on You, and in Your name, we have come against this vast army. O Lord, You are our God; do not let man prevail against You'" (2 Chronicles 14:11 NIV).

I love Asa's faith! He declared that it didn't matter if there was trouble on every side and his enemies outnumbered him, because he believed that if God was on his side, all would be well. The Lord struck down their enemies, and they fled, and so the Lord gave them rest on every side (see 2 Chronicles 14:12 and 15: 4, 15).

Are there any words more beautiful to a battle-weary soul? *The Lord fought for them and gave them rest on every side, so that they could build and prosper.* I cried out to the Lord for this promise, and He heard me. I can't say that my adult children are experiencing divine health or freedom from every trial, but I can say that we have peace and rest in the midst of the ongoing healing process. As we are learning to trust Him in spite of adversity, we are building and prospering. Our marriage, at its 51st anniversary, is strong. The Lord is teaching our adult children and their children. God is our provider. Rest is our portion.

It's all yours for the asking. "The Lord's unfailing love surrounds the one who trusts in Him" (Psalm 32:10 NIV). I survived by clinging to His living words as I would cling to a rock in the sea while the waves of fear beat upon me. I knew that if I could just hold on to my heavenly Father's Word and trust in His good heart, I wouldn't drown. I claimed Scripture, even when the adversary shouted failure and death, when I couldn't see a breakthrough. And, I called others to pray for our family.

The apostle Paul declared, "We were under great pressure, far beyond our ability to endure, so that we despaired even of life. Indeed, in our hearts we felt the sentence of death. But this happened that we might not rely on ourselves but on God, Who raises the dead. He has delivered us from such a deadly peril, and He will deliver us. In Him we have set our hope that He will continue to deliver us, as you help us by your prayers. Then many will give thanks on our behalf for the gracious favor granted us in answer to the prayers of many" (2 Corinthians 1:8-11 NIV).

Restercise:

Spend time meditating on the promises of God. You may want to write out your favorites and put them on "3-by-5" cards for easy memory or in your journal. It helps to post them where you can see them and remember His word to you. The Bible tells us His Word is a shield and a sword. Stand on it! It's more certain than what we see or feel. It can move mountains.

My friend, Patti, asks the Lord to give her a melody to sing the Scripture promises. When you feel beleaguered by fear and problems, singing a praise chorus or hymn is a wonderful way to lift your spirit.

Like King Asa, in what area of your life would you like to experience rest on every side (so you could build and prosper)?

_____

_____

God is for you! All of heaven is for you, for you are God's beloved. Look up! Your Redeemer and your redemption draw near.

Praying a Puritan prayer:
> "O Lord God, You are my protecting arm, fortress, refuge, shield, and buckler. Fight for me, and my foes must flee; uphold me, and I cannot fall; strengthen me, and I stand unmovable; equip me, and I shall receive no wound; stand by me, and Satan will depart; anoint my lips with a song of salvation, and I shall shout Your victory."
>
> *The Valley of Vision: A Collection of Puritan Prayers and Devotions*, edited by Arthur Bennet, 1975, page 37

Scripture Focus and Words of Wisdom

"[Our] faith is strengthened as [we] keep the promises of God before [us] and consider not the difficulties in the way of the things promised, but the character and resources of God Who has made the promises."
—Paul Little (reference: Romans 4:20-22)

"They who dwell in the shelter of the Most High will rest in the shadow of the Almighty. 'Because *they* love Me,' says the Lord, 'I will rescue them and protect them for they acknowledge My name. They will call upon Me, and I will answer them and be with them in trouble. I will deliver them and honor them. With a long life I'll satisfy them and show them my salvation'" (Psalm 91:1, 14-16 NIV).

"In worship we meet the power of God and stand in its strengthening."
—Nels F.S. Ferre (1769-1821) Swedish American Theologian

DAY 29:
Traits of the Secure Child of God

In the 18 years since my burnout experience, and with the lessons my Heavenly Father taught me, I have made it my goal to think and act like a secure child of God—all by His enabling and grace.

Orphan thinking and behaviors may try to manifest as I continue on my wellness journey, but I now know the difference between orphan thinking and resting within the arms of God. I've learned to trust Him with all the people and things I've tried to protect. This lists how secure children of God feel in their hearts and, therefore; how they think:

1. They know they have a protective, loving, heavenly Father, and that He cherishes them. They return His love with a heart of gratitude.

2. They have an intimate relationship with Jesus, their Savior and righteousness.

3. They abide in the Word of God and feed their spirit by listening to, reflecting on, and journaling about what God is teaching them.

4. They take time for beauty and nature, for rest and play.

5. They give themselves permission to get healthy, even when others around them are sick.

6. They choose life at all times and know that the joy of the Lord is their strength.

7. When sad, they ask for God's comfort and grace, by running into His arms.

8. They keep open hands, surrendering what must be released to the Lord and receiving all that He wants to give to them.

9. They allow the Lord to be their defense, to fight their battles. They carry everything to Him.

10. Gratitude, peace, joy, and love—the fruits of the Spirit—are their inheritance.

11. They develop friendships, allowing others to share their joys and sorrows.

12. They love to feed and strengthen God's sheep, including themselves.

13. They fast from self-condemnation and unreasonable self-expectations.

14. They value the approval of God more than the approval of others.

15. They are not pushed or shoved; they walk in a measured pace and are led by the Spirit.

16. They know they can do nothing without abiding in Christ, and they love that.

17. They know they can fail at something and still feel loved. They know God's love is not contingent upon their performance.

18. They have uncluttered hearts and are at peace, centered in the love of the Heavenly Father.

19. They feel no compulsion to impress others, only to delight in God and let His love flow to others. They enjoy people, but they don't need their validation.

20. They are comfortable being alone with God, taking time to listen to God's heart.
21. They allow God to work in them, depending on His strength, wisdom, and anointing.
22. They are responsive to God, not feeling responsible for everything or everyone.
23. They know God is taking care of them, and that He will do the most loving thing.
24. They live without fear; this is the abundant life.
25. They relax in the presence of others and God, because they know they're loved just as they are, not as they think they should be.

Restercise:

As you read the list of traits, did you see yourself? I hope so, for it grieves our Father's heart when we live in fear of abandonment, and it leads to exhaustion and burnout. Let's take up the truth of who we are in Christ and declare these affirmations. This list helped me walk in truth.

1. I choose to trust God to guide my life and the lives of those I love. I'll ask the Lord to expose the motives of my heart, especially any orphan thinking. My fears generate control, panic, and rescuing. I'll repent of fear and keep my eyes on Jesus, the Author and Finisher of my faith.

2. I choose to lay down the fear of loss. God has everyone I love in His hand (see John 10:29).

3. I am not responsible for saving the world, including my adult children and other family members. I will pray instead and be led by love, sharing my testimony when God opens the door. I will be responsive to the Holy Spirit and remember that God is responsible, willing, and able. Jesus Christ is the Savior of the world.

4. I have all the time I need to do the will of God and to play and create. He is not a harsh taskmaster. His burden is light.

5. I will give out of the overflow of the Holy Spirit's infilling and enabling. I will check in with my body to see if it's tired and take naps and retreats when needed.

6. I'll remember that Jesus has a "chariot of joy and comfort" for everyone who looks to Him. I can trust Him to provide and save them.

7. My goal is not to live to make others happy through codependency, but to point them to God, their Provider and Joy-giver.

8. I'll fly solo without the weight of trying to carry others. I can't fly for others. They must use their own wings. We are each accountable to Him. He loves us one-on-one, face-to-face, and heart-to-heart. I can care but not carry. God will carry them on His wings, His shoulders. His watchful eye is on every sparrow.

9. I give myself permission to get well, to be whole and joyful. This will encourage my family and friends, even those who are sick. I will pray and invite Jesus to heal all of us.

10. I release all my regrets for my mistakes and sins, believing the cross of Christ is big enough to cover me and the sins of this world. I forgive myself, because Jesus has forgiven me. He said that He would make all things new.

11. I'll remember if it's not light, it's not right. When I'm asked to do something by or for someone, I'll check in with my heart to determine if I'm being led by love or by guilt and fear. If love leads me, I'll enjoy peace and have God's grace in the doing. If any wrong motive leads me, I'll become depleted.

12. I'm committed to abiding in Christ, the author of rest, peace, and joy. I only bear big fruit for His kingdom by abiding in Him and trusting Him to teach me.

"Jesus, I Am Resting"

Jesus, I am resting, resting in the joy of what Thou art.

I am finding out the greatness of Thy loving heart.

Thou hast bid me gaze upon Thee, and Thy beauty fills my soul.

For by Thy transforming power, Thou hast made me whole.

Ever lift Thy face upon me, as I work and wait for Thee.

Resting 'neath Thy smile, Lord Jesus, earth's dark shadows flee.

Brightness of my Father's glory, sunshine of my Father's face,

Keep me ever trusting, resting. Fill me with Thy grace.

Hymn by Jean Pigott and J. Mountain

Prayer:

Jesus, You have said, "Come with Me, by yourself, to a quiet place, and get some rest." Lord Jesus, I breathe in Your loving presence. I love You. Hold my heart in Your hand. Walk within me upon the furrows and the yet-unplowed areas of my heart. Soften the soil with Your footprints, and then sow truth so that I may be fruitful for the sake of Your Kingdom.

I kiss Your pierced hands and place them on my cheeks, and I am consoled. Your kiss upon my brow makes me cry, because I know that You love me. I am fully Yours; let there be nothing between us.

All looks beautiful, restful to me, because You love me. I have time… time to place a fragrant flower on my desk, light a candle, put on music, look up into the open sky, smile at You, and breathe. Behold, I see You smiling back at me. In Your precious name, Jesus, I pray.

Scripture Focus and Words of Wisdom

"You are not an orphan... I will come to you whenever you need Me. You are not comfortless, desolate, or helpless. I, the God of all comfort, comfort you. I give you the Counselor, the Spirit of Truth to be with you and to live in you. Because I live, you will live also. I am in My Father, and you are in Me, and I am in you. Even though the world doesn't see Me, you will see Me" (John 14:16-18, author's paraphrase).

"For most men the world is centered in self, which is misery; to have one's world centered in God is peace."
—Donald Hankey (1874-1917)

"What is 'resting in God,' but the instinctive movement and upward glance of the spirit to Him; the confiding of all one's griefs and fears to Him, and feeling strengthened, patient, hopeful in the act of doing so! It implies a willingness that He should choose for us, a conviction that the ordering of all that concerns us is safer in His hands than in our own."
—James D. Burns, quoted in *The Treasury of David* by Charles H. Spurgeon, vol.1, page 184

DAY 30:
Refilling

In their book, *The Worn-Out Woman,* authors Steve Stephens and Alice Gray write, "If your schedule is too full, you are hardworking, generous. You are probably the kind of person who is willing to give up your piece of dessert if there is not enough to go around. If someone needs a favor, you do it, even if helping means setting aside what you wanted to do. If it comes to making dreams come true, you may lavish your time and money on others while your own precious dreams remain only longings. Your schedule has been too full. Spoonful by spoonful, you generously give away your oil. You are truly a wonder, and we love it that you are so tenderhearted and kind. But, dear one, only a little oil is left in your lamp, and we worry that you are burning out before you find the places where God meant your light to shine."

Beloved of God, daily give yourself permission to get well and to be rested, a vessel full of the Holy Spirit. Continue to learn of His unconditional love.

Listed below are more strategies for refilling. Prayerfully consider and apply each one.

1. Delegating: When you feel overwhelmed with tasks, consider what you can reassign to another. (Who has the grace, anointing and willingness to do it?)
2. Protect soul-nurturing time, and set healthy boundaries.

3. Read good books that inspire you, strengthen you, and remind you of God's love: The Bible, devotionals, personal experience stories, and others.

4. Journal: let not your heart be troubled (see John 14:1). Write it out. Talk to God, pray it out, and allow Him talk to you.

5. Forgive others *and yourself* frequently; God does. God only wants your availability to forgive; He will be your ability. Regret is a poison, a pathway for the enemy to discourage you. Look forward to Christ's words: "Behold, I make all things new" (Revelation 21:5 NKJ).

6. Hebrews 4:6 declares that obedience is the door to rest. When hearing His voice, don't harden your heart, but believe, listen, and respond to Him.

7. Sabbath rest (Hebrews 4:10): resting from our own work will enable us to enter God's rest, as God rested from His work on the Sabbath. Naps are good!

8. Discover your strengths, passions, and dreams. Make time to pursue them, even if only in small steps. This will lead to strength and joy.

9. Let God comfort you. We feel that God is proudest of us when we "do good" but is disappointed in us when we feel we've failed or feel afraid, grieving, or angry. *This is orphan thinking.* Ask Him to comfort you, forgive you, and help you; ask for His grace and courage to endure. He is never disappointed with you. You will never know Him fully as the "God of All Comfort" if you don't ask for His comfort when you need it most.

10. Pray for His perspective and firsthand grace. Seeing through His eyes with an eternal perspective invites rest.

11. Rest with a favorite worship CD.

12. Organize your space; clear clutter to make room for new enjoyable things to enter your life.
13. Feed yourself and your family a healthy meal or snack.
14. Turn off the negative news, as it adds stress and fatigue. Instead, focus on the happy things around you and in this world. Read Philippians 4:8.
15. Explore your creative side: paint, play a musical instrument, or try a new hobby. Exploring your creativity stimulates your mind, increases enthusiasm, and releases endorphins.
16. Laugh! Watch a funny movie, read funny stories, and post funny pictures. Danny Kay in "The Court Jester," and "I Love Lucy" reruns are my favorites.
17. Get a good night of sleep, at least 8 hours. Keep your sleep area dark to reduce any disruptions. I use an eye cover.
18. Cuddle up with the kids, a puppy, or a spouse.
19. Call your mom, dad, mentor, sister, or best friend to talk things through.
20. Play happy music, and dance around the house.
21. Happiness is a choice. Decide to be grateful. Decide to enjoy the hour, and put all worry away.
22. Commit to slowing down, even stopping for 15 minutes to check in with your heart, body, and your Lord. Then listen. Ask yourself the question, "How can I better nourish myself, feed my spirit, encourage my soul, and enjoy the beauty God has placed around me?"
23. While driving, washing dishes, and cleaning, listen to great audiobooks, an audio Bible, or uplifting music.
24. Improve your view: attach a piece of your child's art, beautiful postcard, photo, favorite vacation spot, or dream trip on a

bulletin board. Place fresh-cut flowers around the house in the various places you work.

25. Sunshine—just twenty minutes a day of outdoor light—improves mood and energy levels.

26. Declare a do-nothing day or hour. Also, declare a "no condemnation" day to go along with it for doing nothing. Live carefree for an hour, or as long as you can... even a lifetime.

27. Light candles.

28. Take a purposeful bath by washing away daily cares. Make it therapeutic and calming with scented bath salts and essential oils. Don't forget the music, the lights down low... and candles. P.S. Don't fall asleep in the tub.

29. Work with your hands, and it will free up your mind: paint, make crafts, build, rebuild, learn to play a musical instrument, or garden.

30. Box clean: put the box in the center of the room you are in. Put everything in the box that needs to be put away. Hide the box until you can get to it. If you can't get to it, oh well—you didn't need it, or you'll buy another.

31. Sip your way to serenity: enjoy your favorite tea or hot drink. Sit down with a cup of tea and savor it. Herbal teas like chamomile are best for relaxation.

32. Have a date with yourself and only yourself. Goof off, wander... stroll around a bookstore, art store, gardens or museum. Take your journal, find a comfortable spot to write, and share your heart on paper.

33. Set aside a personal getaway space indoors or out to serve as a haven, a resting spot, a place to unwind and put your feet up, to pray, daydream, recharge, or to be in your own sanctuary. Outdoors: add a hammock or swing, perhaps a pot of fragrant

flowers. In the bedroom, add soft sheets, a perfect pillow, a plump duvet, flowers, candles, and music. Add a reading spot with perfect light. Create a personal altar where you go to pray. Decorate a dresser top, a small table, or a shelf with symbolic items of rest, peace, and worship.

34. Grow something. Find beauty and refreshment in your own backyard or in the indoor plants.

35. Get a massage.

36. Enroll in a fun class. It's refreshing! Dance, writing, art, photography, cooking, sculpture, foreign language, and bird watching are a few of the endless opportunities available.

37. Play with the kids or pets. Romp! Read them a book. Tell them a story of your own life.

38. Listen to soothing music with an easy tempo. Pleasing music increases brain waves associated with relaxation and decreases heart rate and blood pressure.

39. Visit the neighbors you hardly know, and take a treat: cookies, muffins, your extra garden produce, etc. Giving kindness will relax you. Take the kids so they can see love in action.

40. Eliminate half of your activities for one week. Call it a sabbatical.

41. Lie on the grass with the children or by yourself; watch the clouds or stars.

42. Do a fun puzzle (leave it out) or pull out the Scrabble game. Start a poem on the refrigerator with magnetic word pieces, and watch it grow as others contribute.

43. Take a walk: a 10-minute brisk walk will increase your energy level for up to two hours. Carefree walking can improve memory, reduce anxiety and refresh you. Take a gratitude walk—not for exercise, not to plan your day, but just to see God's hand in every flower and tree, just to be part of His beautiful handwork.

44. Pour into your life as much as you pour out.

45. Mentors, counselors, and life coaches—use them!

46. Silence and solitude (contemplation and reflection) help us to listen to our own heart and God's heart, to see ourselves apart from the roles we play.

47. "Let not your heart be troubled" (John 14:1 NKJ). Getting at the root of our fears of abandonment will help us displace those fears with the truth that God will never leave us or forsake us. God can and will give us a peace that passes understanding.

48. When in doubt, wait on the Lord. Remember, God's wisdom is pure, peaceable, and easy to receive. Follow green lights, open doors, and peace. Follow Jesus—the giver of joy!

49. Choose life every time! Goodness and mercy shall follow you.

50. Determine to be happy and enjoy life. Have an attitude of gratitude. See the cup half full. Imagine the best, not the worst. Nourish your life.

51. Connect with your generals (those who have gone before and know the way to wholeness) and counselors (people of rest and peace). Make an appointment with them. Bother them! Really, they will consider it a blessing. See Titus 2:4.

52. Three times a day, Daniel prayed. This is how he had the faith to trust the Lord while in the lion's den. Check in with Jesus, and just be His.

53. Take time to say to yourself: "I have time!" I have all the time I need to do the will of the Father, because He holds time in His hands. I have time to rest and play, because it's God's will for me to be healthy.

54. Ask God to turn sight (what you see) into insight (what you can learn).

55. Choose to walk in the Spirit. It's as easy as getting into a car. Just declare that you will walk in the Spirit today by trusting in the Lord's leading.

56. Remember that you can do all things from within the circumference of the loving arms of Father God. "God is for you, and since He is for you, who can be against you and win? You are more than a conqueror in Christ Jesus, Who loves you, and nothing can separate you from the love of God that is in Christ Jesus, our Lord" (adapted from Romans 8:31, 37-39).

My Rest Confession:

I give myself permission to get well. I remember God loves me; He will do the most loving thing for my loved ones and for me. He is for me, so none can prosper who are against me. I shall be still—like a flat-bottomed vase—resting on a firm foundation in Christ. I say *no* to striving and trying to meet the burdensome expectations of others. I shall refill to overflowing, giving only out of the overflow, never to be spilled out or dried out. All I do will be prompted by Him and for Him, from a place of abiding in Christ, within the circle of His loving arms.

I renounce orphan thinking. I am no longer alone. I'm born of God. I have a Heavenly Father Who will take care of the world and me. He is responsible. I get to be responsive to Him. Abba loves me and keeps me in His hand at all times. He will teach me all things, lovingly correct me, lead me, anoint me, and help me to finish my call. He will strengthen me. He will fill me with peace and courage.

My future is full of hope, goodness, and mercy. I have time to do the will of God. I can rest and wait on Him. I resign from all rescuing behaviors inspired by fear. I will wait, listen to Abba's heart, and be unafraid; He is always with me and will never abandon me. I'm blessed at all times. My seed is blessed to 1,000 generations. I can do all things Christ has desired for me to do, for He enables me. I can rest and play without guilt. I can dance, create a garden, and sit in it to enjoy the fragrance of flowers and the beauty of hummingbirds. I can just be God's own dear child without a duty to perform, a backpack to carry, or a to-do list. This is God's desire for me: to be carefree, to love Him, to be mindful of Him, grateful for all He's done for me, and to be in constant relationship with Him. When in grief or pain, I can ask for the comfort of the Holy Spirit to fill me. As a child rests in her dad's arms, I can pat His face and wrap my arms around His neck.

This is my first call: to love God with all my heart, soul, mind, and strength. In this comes my healing, wholeness, and abundant life. Only then will I have anything of Him to give to others; only then can I fully love others. Underneath me are the everlasting arms. Jesus Christ gave His life for me and lives in my heart. **I am a safe and secure child of God.**

GOING DEEPER:
Questions for reflection, discussion, and journaling

Additional discussion questions for each day's devotional begin next. They delve deeper into the roots of our fatigue and burnout tendencies. These questions are designed to expose the heart-level messages that lead to the unending cycle of rescuing and over-committing. They help initiate study group conversations, couple sharing, and individuals wanting to interact with their prayer journals. As people tell their stories, or through journaling, we learn life lessons that help us grow and heal. Be sure and check out the Going Deeper questions for more revelation.

If you are in a group, read and respond to these questions prior to the group meetings. It will give you time to think about an answer and feel prepared. Choose the questions that fit your time limit and interest for discussion. You may want to bring your Bible to the group and/or look up recommended scriptures before meetings.

This study is set up for a five-day week, lasting six weeks. It could last eight weeks with week one as an introduction to the topic and getting-to-know you meeting. The eighth week can be a celebration meeting, with testimonies and sharing of what group members have gained from their interaction with the book and each other. It can be customized, timewise, any way a person, couple, or group desires. Prayerfully invite the Holy Spirit to lead you. He is the Counselor and the Spirit of Truth. He will be with you both now and forever (see John 14:16-17, 26).

GOING DEEPER QUESTIONS: DAYS 1-5

DAY 1: How and Where it All Began

» In what ways can you identify with Gena's story? Look at the list of traits of the orphan heart on pages xvii-xviii. What surprised you on that list?

» What in life is causing you the most stress right now, potentially leading you into burnout? (Refer to the hat *restercise* activity on page 3.)

» On page xxii, what characteristics of burnout could you identify within yourself?

» Read Matthew 11:28-30 in several versions aloud. In what ways do you find this Scripture comforting?

» Discuss the word "yoke" in your group and share what it may look like or mean to you.

DAY 2: Let Me Take Care of You

» Joyce Meyer said, "I have found that when I am doing something that doesn't give me joy anymore, that's a strong indication God is finished with that thing, and I need to be ready for something new." She goes on to say, "When you can sense that the grace of God is no longer with you to do something or that the joy you felt is gone, don't just complain and continue until you end up burned-out. Have the courage to say, 'I did things this way for a long time, but I believe God is leading me to do something else.'" (*Battlefield of the Mind Bible*, 2017, page 1623, quote by Joyce Meyer). Where has the grace lifted in the activities of your life?

» Do an activity inventory. In what ways could you change those activities to restore your joy and grace?

If they cannot be changed right now, ask God for His grace to endure and be a blessing while you wait for revelation on what to change. Sometimes, it's just a matter of getting God's perspective. He gives grace to press on.

» The Apostle Paul left the mission of building the church at Ephesus after three years. (See Acts 20:22.) Why did he leave? What do you think he knew about what was coming next?

» It's been said that we give power to something when we're afraid of it. That's why Jesus said, "Fear not!" Name something you are afraid of at this time in your life.

» Ask God for His truth and ask others for prayer to unseat any fear.

DAY 3: Black and white Thinking

- It's not what I can do *for* God, but what I do *in* Him, by abiding *in* Him. It's not about being brave and strong *for* Him, *for I am terrified at times*. It's learning to be brave and strong *in* Him. Identify a significant thing, or things, you would like to do *in* God, allowing Him to work by His Spirit *through* you.

Ask for prayer support in taking this step. Begin to see Jesus with you in all you do. He is for you and ever ready to help you. Practice this week resting in His provision, wisdom, and love.

- Where or when in your life have you had black and white thinking?

Describe that situation and outcome. If you have black and white thinking now, share your fears. Ask for prayer support for the difficult decision ahead.

- When I was a child, one of my favorite games was Hot Potato. We used to pretend a ball or a bean bag was a hot potato. One person in a group would start the game and throw the ball into someone's hands. That person would quickly toss it to another before it burned their hands. The game would go on with hilarity until the ball (hot potato) was dropped. Similarly, when life or Satan throws you a hot potato: a fear, worry, a problem, toss it quickly to Jesus. He can handle the heat. What hot potatoes would you like to give to God today?

- Scriptures to bring rest: Psalm 62:1, Isaiah 40:31, Psalm 46:10. At home, remember to take time to sit quietly and let God love you.

DAY 4: Be Responsive, Not Responsible

» If you wear the "I'm Responsible" T-shirt, you have probably put your own needs and feelings last, or locked away. What would you like to do for yourself if you had the time and freedom from caretaking others?

List ways to fill up and restore your body and soul.

Share the list and ask for prayer.

» Who would you like to see Jesus putting His arm around? Is there someone who piles big expectations on you?

» Are you that someone, piling performance expectations on yourself?

» We can unwittingly put our own or other people's expectations of us before God and His expectations. The Bible calls that idolatry. When we repent of trying to please others, we become free to be concerned only about pleasing God. His expectations of us are purely loving. He is not the author of weighty burdens.

» Researcher O. Fred Donaldson, author of *Playing by Heart* states, "Play boosts your immune system, steadies and strengthens your cardiovascular system and increases serotonin." In what ways have you forgotten how to play, not given yourself permission to play, or not made time for it? Talk about it.

» Romans 8:14-17 speaks of our being released from fear and slavery. Read this promise and take it into your heart as your own.

DAY 5: Abba Chair, Your Resting Place

» When you were a child, where was your safe place?

» Was there a tree house, fort, Grandma's attic, or other place where you felt happy and carefree? Describe this place. Tell others why it was your safe place.

» Think of a time when you have experienced provision from God in a miraculous way. Share that with the group to build each other's faith. Do you currently need a miracle of God's provision?

Release that to God by asking for prayer. You will feel lifted by the prayer support of others.

» Think of a place of your own choosing where you can rest for 15 minutes or more. A chair? A garden spot? Describe it to the group. It may give them ideas for the restercise assignment.

» In Isaiah 58:11, the Lord promises to make you like a well-watered garden. Read it and soak up the promise.

» What day this week spoke to you the most? Why? Did a quote or scripture impact you?

GOING DEEPER QUESTIONS: DAYS 6-10:

DAY 6: Rest is a Helium Balloon

» Today's restercise questions ask you to identify what lead balloons you carry around. What do you need to let go of?

» What is your greatest fear about letting go?

» Are you willing to surrender all to God? If you desire, ask for prayer support to release those balloons to God.

» What does true rest look like to you? Share with others in your group.

» Can you imagine not having a care in the world, feeling completely at peace, and able to release every need to God? What would that look like for you? Would you be dancing, crying for joy, laughing, or playing?

- » Has God ever spoken to your heart concerning your weariness and burden bearing? What did He say?

- » Scripture: "I'll be a Father to you, and you shall be My sons and daughters," says the Lord God Almighty. (See 2 Corinthians 6:18 NKJ.)
- » Take time to pray for one another.

Day 7: Flat Bottom

- » Talk about the ways you feed your spirit, strengthen your body, and refill.

- » Do you feel guilty when you think about spending time on yourself—to nurture yourself? Can you identify when that thinking began?

- » Ask Jesus if what you have believed is the truth. Listen as He speaks to your heart. What is He saying? Write it down and/or share it. The revelation God gives you can free others, too.

- » What other things could you do or try that would renew your spirit and help you to feel carefree? What are some of the ways you can protect the rest times? For example: write it on your calendar as an appointment.

» Will you give yourself permission to refill, to rest, and to receive? Read 2 Corinthians 4:16.

Day 8: Leap of Faith

» Are there any decisions in your life where you may need to take a leap of faith?

» Share and ask for prayer.

» Have you ever gone to a Christian counselor, retreat, or mentor to get help overcoming a problem: marriage, child rearing, job conflicts, etc. If it was helpful, share to encourage others.

Day 9: If It's Not Light, It's Not Right

» See the Restercise activity on page 49, where you listed your daily and weekly commitments or activities. You noted whether they were light or heavy. Were the lists equally balanced? Are you pouring out more than you are taking in? Brainstorm ways to lighten your load.

» See Isaiah 30:15, 18 to remind you that God waits to help you.

Day 10: One Rotten Plank Sinks the Ship

» Lies we have believed about our worth to God or negative vows we have made need to be broken and replaced with God's truth so we can be free. A vow is a promise we make to ourselves that is motivated by fear, judgment, unforgiveness, negative expectations, anger, or a lack of trust in God. What have you read or heard so far in this study that has changed an orphan heart belief that you've had or exposed a vow you've made?

» Ask the Holy Spirit to replace the lie—the orphan belief—with the truth of God's love for you. "Lord, show me the lie or orphan thought that keeps me tired and replace it with Your truth. The truth is

» Do you have an example of another time when God spoke truth and revelation into your heart that changed you? Perhaps it was when you realized He loved you, or when He saved a relationship, or sovereignly changed the direction of your life.

» What day this week spoke to you the most? Why? Did a quote or scripture impact you?

GOING DEEPER QUESTIONS: DAYS 11-15:

Day 11: No Hats, No Costumes

» Did anything surprise or delight you about the "No Hats, No Costumes" story on page 57?

» Share with the group which roles/costumes you wear each week. Do they all fit? Which ones would you like to take off?

» Which roles do you enjoy? Why?

» Do you have a regular time to read the Bible and pray?

» Share how you find/make time to feed your spirit. What does it mean to you?

» If you don't have Bible/prayer time, share why it's difficult to accomplish. Group members may help you discover what works for them.

» Jesus fed over 5,000 men, plus women and children until they were fully satisfied. He is the Bread of Life. Remind yourself to be daily fed by Him.

Day 12: Some Pay to Climb Mountains

» Did you sketch your mountains? If so, please share to encourage others in your group. If you didn't sketch them, still feel free to identify your mountains, the ones you have angst about scaling. What are your fears?

Ask for prayer.

» Share a favorite scripture that helps you scale mountains or difficulties.

» Read Habakkuk 3:19.

Day 13: Condemnation Fast

» Have you given yourself permission to take a self-condemnation fast? How long did you last? What were the results?

» How did you feel? If you haven't tried it, why not?

Will you try it for a month, a week, a day, forever?

» My daughter, Emily, would remind me to say three nice things about myself after I had criticized myself for failing to do something. If you find yourself criticizing or condemning yourself, try saying three nice things about yourself. It may make you laugh and remember that you are loved. Give yourself the gift of grace as you have given it to others.

» Read Romans 8:1.

Day 14: The Only Way I Fail God

» Would you like prayer support to receive peace for a mistake or failure that continues to bring you sorrow?

» The Word says in James 5:16, that if we confess our sins to one another and pray for each other, we may receive healing. Sometimes, we need reassurance that we are forgiven and therefore cleansed from all regret and grief. Jesus wants you to live shame-free. There is no shame in Jesus, and He dwells in you. Always remember, the cross is big enough to cover the sins of the world.

Day 15: He Loves Me; He Will Do the Most Loving Thing

» What do you fear losing?

» Will you surrender the situation or person fully to God and His safe keeping? It can bring great peace to ask Him to do the most loving thing. Share and receive prayer support.

» Read 2 Timothy 1:12 for reassurance. Write it in your own words.

» What day this week spoke to you the most? Why? Did a quote and scripture impact you?

GOING DEEPER QUESTIONS: DAYS 16-20:

Day 16: Don't Run Away; Run Deeper

» If you could run away from all of life's stresses and problems, where would you go? What would your perfect place look like?

» David described what he would do in Psalm 55: 6-8 (Amplified): "Oh that I had wings like a dove! I would fly away and be at rest. I would wander far away. I would lodge in the peace of the wilderness. I would hurry to my refuge (my tranquil shelter far away) from the stormy wind and from the tempest." How do these places compare with God's loving arms and His Father heart for you?

» Can you escape God's love anywhere you go?

» Read Psalm 139:7-10. Write it in your own words.

Day 17: The Cure for Regret

» Have you found a cure for regret? Explain.

» What helps you to see yourself in the light of Christ's grace?

» An orphan heart only sees her flaws and feels dressed in rags. But those who know they are fully loved as God's children see themselves as clothed in Christ's righteousness. Do you need to exchange how you see yourself with new eyes? Pray and receive.

» Read Isaiah 61:10.

Day 18: Every Trial an Opportunity

» The restercise activity on page 95 asks you if you are worried about someone or something.

» Read 2 Timothy 1:12. Ask for prayer support.

» A prayer box or basket can be a visual reminder that you have placed your prayer request in God's hand. Write it out and release it to the Lord's care.

Day 19: A Pony—A Chariot

» As a child, did you have a special safe place, comforting person or pet, or an activity that felt like Gena's chariot/pony times?

» Pastor Noel spoke of asking for God's grace to endure his wife's health trial. What do you need God's grace to cover in your life and relationships?

» Ask the Lord for His grace and receive it with gratitude.

» Read 2 Thessalonians 2:16-17 for promises of God's love, strength, and grace.

Day 20: The Un-pruned Tree

» Can you identify with Gena's story of sucker branches?

It's helpful to first identify those sucker branches so you can let them go. If you drew a tree representing your life from the restercise activity, share it to encourage others.

» Brainstorm with the group ways to let go of the sucker branches.

» How do you best feed your spirit?

» John 15 tells us to abide in Christ, the true Vine, so that we may bear fruit. What does that mean to you?

» What day this week spoke to you the most? Why? Did a quote or scripture impact you?

GOING DEEPER QUESTIONS: DAYS 21-25:

Day 21: Just in Case Thinking

» What is the attitude of your heart: *just in case* or *just in time*? Explain where and when that attitude started.

» Do you have a God story of when He showed up *just in time*? Share.

Day 22: Permission to Get Well

» The restercise activity on page 116 asks us to identify where our happiness is dependent on a person, job, or anything other than God. Did the Lord speak to you, and would you like prayer to let go of people-pleasing or putting someone/anything before God?

Day 23: If I'm Willing, God Is Able

» Is there anyone you need God's ability to forgive?

» Are you willing to forgive? _____ Forgiveness is a process, and each time we ask for God's grace to forgive, another layer of our heart heals. Eventually, God gives us the ability to pray with genuine concern for those who have hurt us.

» Would you like to ask God for forgiveness, and to forgive those who've hurt you? Freedom awaits right now. Pray silently or with your group, "Lord, forgive me for _____. I receive Your grace and forgiveness because Jesus has paid my sin debt on Calvary. I'm forever grateful. I forgive _____. Grant me continuing grace to forgive all those who have hurt me. I am willing, Lord, because You are my ability. Thank You. In Jesus' name I pray."

» In the Lord's prayer, Jesus told us to pray to forgive others as He has forgiven us.

» Read Matthew 6:12 and Matthew 18:21-22.

Day 24: I Have Time to Do the Will of God

» What a concept: I have time! How did this day's lesson speak to you? Do you believe you have time to do God's will, or to do self-care, or to play?

Self-care and play are part of God's will for you. He wants you healthy and carefree. Will you give yourself permission to be on God's time and trust Him for time?

» Pray together and ask God to free you in the area of time, to find true rest, and His Spirit's abiding presence amidst the minutes of your life.

» Read Hebrews 4:16 to receive His mercy and grace in time of need.

Day 25: Thinking Paper Will Save Me

» This is the age of information overload! With T.V. news 24/7, internet access on multiple devices, books, mail, and podcasts we are inundated with constant media and things to process. Can you identify with information fatigue?

» What do you collect for security?

» You may identify with Gena's perceived safety in paper, only to realize it buries her time and thinking with clutter. What clutters your time and thinking?

» Have you tried a technology/information fast even for one day? Share your experience. Have you ever forgotten your cell phone, then felt lost without it? What does that reveal to you?

» Take the challenge to fast from this world's information, just to give all your attention to the Lord—even for an hour, a day, or a weekend.

» What day this week spoke to you the most? Why? Did a quote or Scripture impact you?

GOING DEEPER QUESTIONS: DAYS 26-30:

Day 26: Hurry Sickness

» Many believe the lie that "if I'm busy, I must be valuable and important." Check in with your heart. In what ways do you believe that lie?

» In what ways does your busyness keep you from living the way you'd love to live? What would your perfect day, week, and life look like if time wasn't an issue?

» Do you have trouble saying "no" to people's requests of you? Why? How could you change your focus from what others want you to do, to what God wants for you? Remember He is gentle and not a harsh taskmaster.

» Sometimes we stay busy to avoid our deepest fears of loss or to try to stay in control of an unpredictable world. If you've overscheduled your life or your children's lives, what may you be avoiding?

» Rest comes by remembering that we are not on our own. We are yoked with Christ's business, not to our busyness. Jesus said to His disciples, in Mark 6:31, "Come away by yourselves to a secluded place and rest a while." When stressed or tired, even five minutes in a quiet room can remind you to breathe and refocus. Can you think of other ways to have a five-minute stress break?

Day 27: Building a Sanctuary

» It has been said that "beauty" is its own healer. What is beautiful to you?

» Do you have a collection of something beautiful?

» Do you like to draw, paint, build, garden, cook, play an instrument, write, etc.? What happens in your heart when you take time to do something creative and beautiful?

Day 28: Rest on Every Side

» Do you have a favorite scripture, hymn, or song you sing when you feel overwhelmed or afraid?

» For me, it was Psalm 34. I would sing this familiar praise song every time my daughter was sick. It addressed my fears perfectly, and gave me peace when I sang, "For I sought the Lord and He heard me and delivered me from all my fears!" God gave King Asa rest on every side so that he could build and prosper. Where do you desire this same blessing? Ask for prayer.

» Read Psalm 34. What line of this Psalm stands out for you?

Day 29: Traits of the Secure Child of God

» See the 25 traits of a secure child of God on page 153. Did you see yourself in those traits?

» What would you like to focus on in this list so that your joy will be full, and to enable you to avoid future burnout?

» See the restercise activity of 12 affirmations on page 156-157. Which ones spoke to you? Are there any you'd like to add that apply to your life? Share with the group.

Day 30: Refilling

» Go to the refilling list on pages 161-167. With your group talk about the 56 strategies for refilling. Consider picking one each week, for the next 6 months, to practice ways to fill up to overflow. Remember, we're to give out of the overflow, never spilling out to empty. Pray for each other to abide in Christ always.

» It has been recommended by Karen Mains, author of *The God Hunt*, to reread this book in six months to see how you've done in maintaining a light and carefree heart. You may need a reminder to "let go and let God." He is your Father and is responsible for you and His world. He's our provider in all ways. You're blessed with being His responsive child through Christ Jesus, our Lord and Savior.

» Thank you for taking this journey with me. I pray for your joy to be full in body, soul, and spirit. Fill up, beloved! It's God's will for your life to be in health and to prosper, even as your soul prospers (3 John: 2). Continue to give yourself permission to get well for you are greatly loved.

LEADER'S GUIDE

I Can't Rest Now, Lord! I'm Responsible... is a Biblically-based 30-day or six to eight-week study designed to bring men and women into the knowledge of God's Father heart, allowing them to relinquish fear and come into rest. Conversation enables deeper understanding as participants share their experiences of knowing God and finding freedom from performing for love and acceptance. On pages 171 through 193, group discussion questions are prepared for every session. In addition to the restercise questions and activities that go with each day's lesson. The questions and activities will facilitate personal sharing of the lives and experiences of group members, with the goal of setting hearts free from a life of exhaustion/burnout. This study is successful in large or small group settings depending on the time allocated for all to share and pray. All ages, backgrounds, and stages of life will enrich the group experience. Groups of six to twelve are ideal, although this book is also wonderful for individual study, prayer partners, or husband and wife teams.

As you share your heart with the group, you will encourage those in your group to also share. You set the example by the transparency and depth of your responses to the questions and the reading of the book. Therefore, it is suggested that you start by sharing first. Once the group has bonded, others may want to jump in first with a revelation or response to the study. Because this study is discussion-based rather than leader-based, it's not necessary to have one specific leader. You may want to have another member of the group look over the questions in advance and prepare to lead. Co-leadership is great, too, because if one has to be absent the other is ready to continue. Co-leaders strengthen their group and each other. Be mindful of the quiet group members by drawing them out and asking them if they have anything they'd like to respond to in the study questions.

Pray for those in your group. Listen to their needs and struggles, and bring all concerns to the Lord at the end of the time together each week. Encourage group members to follow through with the study, to attend the group sessions, to engage with the homework, and to pray for each other during the week. Remember, you don't have to have all the answers. This is God's group and you can rest in the Holy Spirit's leadership. God is responsible to heal the hearts of His children. We get the joy of following the promptings of the Holy Spirit. He leads us by inspiring us with love and peace.

Discussion questions and restercise activities are offered, but may be more than can be covered in a single session. Be flexible. Consider the persons in your group as you make decisions about which questions to discuss. Be confident that God holds you and the group in His hand. He is delighted when we do our heart-work. Pray for His truth and love to set people free. Some questions may be moved to a later time for discussion.

Housekeeping ideas: Have participants sign in with contact information, prepare name tags, and have the books ready. Provide water and refreshments. Introduce yourself and group members. Give information about yourself and ask each person to do the same. They will follow your example. Icebreakers work nicely, too. For example: if you could live anywhere in the world and money was no object, where would you live and why?

Introduce the book and the author to your group. Explain the unique elements of the book. Encourage them to journal during the week by interacting with the daily lessons, restercise activities, and *going deeper* questions. And of course, encourage all to read the assigned number of days/lessons. Be prepared to participate. Remind participants that everything discussed in your group will be kept confidential. Open and close groups in prayer. You will be blessed by the group experience.

NOTES

DAY 1:

Saint Augustine quoted by Harvey D. Egan, *An anthology of Christian Mysticism,* (Collegeville, MN: The Liturgical Press, 1996), 61.

DAY 2:

James Hudson Taylor, *Hudson Taylor and The China Inland Mission: Volume 2: The Growth of a Work of God* (Amazon Digital Services LLC, 2010), 43.

DAY 3:

Charles Spurgeon, *Morning by Morning: The Devotions of Charles Spurgeon,* (Grand Rapids, MI: Zondervan, 2008), 16.

Angelus Silesius quoted by Harvey D. Egan, *An Anthology of Christian Mysticism,* (Collegeville, MN: The Liturgical Press, 1996), 521.

DAY 4:

Catherine Jackson, *The Christian's Secret of a Happy Life for Today, A Paraphrase of Hannah Whitall Smith's Classic,* (Old Tappan, New Jersey: Fleming H. Revell Company, 1979).

L.B. Cowman, *Streams in the Desert*, (Grand Rapids, Michigan: Zondervan Publishing House, 1997), September 3.

DAY 5:

C. S. Lewis, *Letters to Malcolm: Chiefly on Prayer,* (Orlando, FL: Mariner Books, 2002), 93.

Charles Haddon Spurgeon, *Morning and Evening,* (CreateSpace Independent Publishing Platform, 2018), 102.

Thomas Kempis quoted by Bob Kelly, *Worth Repeating: More Than 5,000 Classic and Contemporary Quotes,* (Grand Rapids, MI: Kregel Publications, 2003), 155.

DAY 6:

George Mueller, *The Life of Trust*, 1st published in 1861, (University of Michigan Library 2001).

DAY 7:

Christina Rossetti quoted by Emma Mason, *Christina Rossetti: Poetry, Ecology, Faith,* (Oxford, UK:Oxford University Press, 2018), 88.

A. W. Tozer, *Tozer on Worship and Entertainment,* (Camp Hill, PA: WingSpread Publishers, 2006), chapter 6.

DAY 8:

Dietrich Bonhoeffer, *The Cost of Discipleship,* (New York, NY: Simon & Shuster), 56.

DAY 9:

Hudson Taylor and Geraldine Taylor, *Hudson Taylor's Spiritual Secret,* (Incense House Publishing, 2013), 1.

DAY 10:

Abbe Henry de Tourville, *The NIV Maranatha Worship Bible,* (Zondervan Publishing House, 2000) 886 sidebar.

DAY 11:

William James, *The William James Reader* [eBook], (Start Publishing LLLC, 2012).

DAY 12:

John Stanko, consultant, coach, author: www.purposequest.com.

DAY 13:

Luci Shaw quoted by Adele Ahlberg Calhoun, *Spiritual Disciplines Handbook: Practices that Transform Us,* (Downers Grove, IL: InterVarsity Press), 142.

DAY 14:

Catherine Jackson, *The Christian's Secret of a Happy Life for Today: Paraphrase of Hannah Whitall Smith's Classic* (1979).

Jeremy Taylor, *The Rule and Exercises of Holy Living Together with Prayers Containing the Whole Duty of a Christian* (Accessed through Google Books), 199.

DAY 15:

Madame de La Mothe Guyon quoted by Thomas C. Upham, *Life Religious Opinions and Experience of Madame De La Mothe Guyon,* (London, UK: Sampson Low, Son and Co., 1858), 306.

Day16:

Julian of Norwich [translated by Edmund Colledge and James Walsh], *The Life of the Soul: The Wisdom of Julian of Norwich,* (Mahwah, NJ: Paulist Press, 1996), 15.

John Powell, S.J., *Happiness Is an Inside Job,* (Thomas Moore Publisher, 1989), 105.

DAY 17:

John Newton quoted by Jim Jacobs, *From Light into the Abyss: Swindling, Web-Cams, College Youth Behaving Badly,* (Bloomington, IN: Author House, 2016).

Henri J.M. Nouwen, *The Inner Voice of Love,* (Doubleday/Random House Inc., 1998).

DAY 18:

Hannah Whitall Smith, *The Christian's Secret of a Happy Life*, (Barbour Publishing, Inc., 1875 first edition), also quoted in the NIV Maranatha Worship Bible (2000), sidebar 1150.

DAY 19:

Charles R. Swindoll, *The Grace Awakening: Believing in Grace Is One Thing. Living it Is Another,* (Nashville, TN: Thomas Nelson, Inc., 2010), 39.

Charles H. Spurgeon, *Evening by Evening,* (Gainesville, FL: Bridge-Logos, 2005), 131.

DAY 20:

Jerry Bridges, *Disciplines of Grace,* (NavPress, 1991).

Brené Brown Ph.D., *The Gifts of Imperfection*, (Hazelden Publishing, 2010).

DAY 21:

Martin Luther [compiled by Ray Comfort], *Luther Gold,* (Alachua, FL: Bridge Logos, 2009), 50.

Thomas á Kempis, quoted in *The New Book of Christian Quotations*, [compiled by Tony Castle], (New York: Crossroad, 1982), 102.

DAY 22:

John Stanko, consultant, coach, author: www.purposequest.com.

DAY 23:

Oswald Chambers, *My Utmost for His Highest,* (Grand Rapids, MI: Discovery House Publishers, 1992).

St. Jean Baptiste Marie Vianney, The Life of St. Jean Baptiste Marie Vianney, (L'Osservatore Romano, 2005), 5.

Eleanor Roosevelt, *You Learn by Living*, (New York: Harper & Brothers Publishers, 1960).

DAY 24:

Bernie Siegel, MD., Surgeon, Speaker, Author. Best-selling book: *Love, Medicine and Miracles*, (Quill Publisher, 1986).

Andy Stanley, Pastor of North Point Community Church, Alpharetta, Georgia. North Point Ministries.

DAY 25:

John Eldredge, *Moving Mountains: Praying with Passion, Confidence, and Authority, Study Guide,* (Nelson Books, 2016), 21.

DAY 26:

Socrates quoted by Gary Chapman, *Love as a Way of Life: Seven Keys to Transforming Every Aspect of Your Life,* (New York, NY: Doubleday, 2008), 23.

L.B. Cowman, *Streams in the Desert*, (Grand Rapids, Michigan: Zondervan Publishing House, 1997), 336.

DAY 27:

John Wesley, *The Works of the Rev. John Wesley in Ten Volumes: Volume V,* (New York, NY: J. & J. Harper, 1830), 174.

DAY 28:

Paul Little, *How to Give Away Your Faith,* (Downers Grove, IL: InterVarsity Press, 1988), 177.

DAY 29:

Donald Hankey quoted by Martin H, Manser, *The Westminster Collection of Christian Quotations,* (Louisville, KY: Westminster John Knox Press, 2001), 337.

NOTE: *Every effort has been made to note the ownership of these quotes and copyright items. I would be grateful to have further acknowledgments and adjustments in future reprints.* —GB

RECOMMENDED READING:

Anderson, Fil. *Running on Empty: Contemplative Spirituality for Overachievers.* Waterbrook Press, 2004

Andersen, Linda. *Interludes: A Busy Woman's Invitation to Personal and Spiritual Rest.* Waterbrook, 2001

Curtis, Brent, and John Eldredge. *The Sacred Romance: Drawing Closer to the Heart of God.* Nashville, TN: Thomas Nelson, 1997

Dillow, Linda. *Calm My Anxious Heart: A Woman's Guide to Contentment.* Colorado Springs, CO: Navpress, 1998

Davis, Deanna, PH.D. *Living with Intention: Designing a Wildly Fulfilling Remarkable Successful Life.* AuthorHouse, 2005

Farrar, Steve and Mary. *Overcoming Overload: Seven Ways to Find Rest in Your Chaotic World.* Sisters, OR: Multnomah, 2003

Meyer, Joyce. *Help Me, I'm Stressed.* Harrison House, 1998

Rubietta, Jane. *Grace Points: Growth and Guidance in Times of Change.* Downers Grove, Illinois: InterVarsity Press, 2004

Rubietta, Jane, *Still Waters: Finding the Place Where God Restores Your Soul.* Minneapolis, Minnesota: Bethany House Publishers, 1999

Stephens, Steve and Gray, Alice. *The Worn-Out Woman: When Your Life Is Full and Your Spirit Is Empty.* Multnomah Pub. Inc., 2004

Thomas, Kim. *Even God Rested: Why It's Okay for Women to Slow Down* Eugene, OR: Harvest House, 2003

Weaver, Joanna. *Having a Mary Heart in a Martha World.* Revised. Colorado Springs, CO: Waterbrook, 2002

ABOUT THE AUTHOR

Gena Bradford writes for the inspirational market, gently reminding weary, beleaguered women and men of their immeasurable worth to God. A former struggler with burnout, she shares vibrant, life-changing lessons, helping others come into God's rest amid the relentless, everyday challenges of working and living. God loves rested sheep! They are winsome witnesses to a tired, discouraged, and hungry-for-rest world.

Gena's articles have appeared in magazines and anthologies, including: *Guideposts Magazine, Miracles Still Happen, What I Learned from God While Cooking, So Many Miracles, A Cup of Comfort Devotional for Women, Life Savors: Savory Stories to Inspire Your Soul, Love and Forgiveness,* and *Love is A Verb.* A retired teacher in public education, she's currently a part-time adjunct at Whitworth University. Gena enjoys leading worship, as well as keynoting at conferences, retreats, banquets, and training events, stateside and abroad.

Married for 50 years, Gena and Jack delight in their four children and four grandchildren. They live in the Inland Northwest.

To order a book, and for a list of her speaking/teaching topics, or for more information, contact her at:

Gena Bradford
restnow1418@gmail.com
gena@genabradford.com

Genabradford.com

Order additional copies from the author or on *Amazon.com*